The Power of the Maha-Mantra

What is So Special About Chanting Hare Krishna

By
Stephen Knapp

Dedicated to
All seekers looking for the deepest spiritual truth,
and to my own spiritual master who gave such truth to me,
Srila A. C. Bhaktivedanta Swami Prabhupada.

Copyright © 2018, by Stephen Knapp

All rights reserved. No part of this book may be reproduced without written permission from the copyright owner and publisher, except for brief quotations for review or educational purposes.

COVER PHOTO: Beads made from the sacred Tulasi plant, often used for chanting the Hare Krishna maha-mantra in japa or personal meditation, draped over the most revered text of *Srimad-Bhagavatam*, known to give the extraordinary knowledge of the pastimes of the Supreme Lord Sri Krishna, and about the potency of the Hare Krishna maha-mantra.

ISBN-10: 1983873489
ISBN-13: 978-1983873485

Published by
The World Relief Network,
Detroit, Michigan

You can find out more about Stephen Knapp and his books, free ebooks, research, and numerous articles and photos, along with many other spiritual resources at:

www.Stephen-Knapp.com
http://stephenknapp.info
http://stephenknapp.wordpress.com

Other books by the author:

1. The Secret Teachings of the Vedas: The Eastern Answers to the Mysteries of Life
2. The Universal Path to Enlightenment
3. The Vedic Prophecies: A New Look into the Future
4. How the Universe was Created and Our Purpose In It
5. Toward World Peace: Seeing the Unity Between Us All
6. Facing Death: Welcoming the Afterlife
7. The Key to Real Happiness
8. Proof of Vedic Culture's Global Existence
9. The Heart of Hinduism: The Eastern Path to Freedom, Enlightenment and Illumination
10. The Power of the Dharma: An Introduction to Hinduism and Vedic Culture
11. Vedic Culture: The Difference it can Make in Your Life
12. Reincarnation & Karma: How They Really Affect Us
13. The Eleventh Commandment: The Next Step for Social Spiritual Development
14. Seeing Spiritual India: A Guide to Temples, Holy Sites, Festivals and Traditions
15. Crimes Against India: And the Need to Protect its Ancient Vedic Tradition
16. Destined for Infinity, a spiritual adventure in the Himalayas
17. Yoga and Meditation: Their Real Purpose and How to Get Started
18. Avatars, Gods and Goddesses of Vedic Culture: Understanding the Characteristics, Powers and Positions of the Hindu Divinities
19. The Soul: Understanding Our Real Identity
20. Prayers, Mantras and Gayatris: A Collection for Insights, Protection, Spiritual Growth, and Many Other Blessings
21. Krishna Deities and Their Miracles: How the Images of Lord Krishna Interact with Their Devotees.
22. Defending Vedic Dharma: Tackling the Issues to Make a Difference.
23. Advancements of Ancient India's Vedic Culture.
24. Spreading Vedic Traditions Through Temples.
25. The Bhakti-yoga Handbook: A Guide to Beginning the Essentials of Devotional Yoga
26. Lord Krishna and His Essential Teachings
27. Mysteries of the Ancient Vedic Empire.
28. Casteism in India
29. Ancient History of Vedic Culture
30. A Complete Review of Vedic Literature
31. Bhakti-Yoga: The Easy Path of Devotional Yoga

CONTENTS

CHAPTER ONE: 3
MANTRA-YOGA: A NECESSITY FOR THIS AGE

CHAPTER TWO: 10
THE OM MANTRA
   Om Meditation Technique

CHAPTER THREE: 19
THE POWER OF THE MAHA-MANTRA: HOW IT WORKS

CHAPTER FOUR: 30
THE IMPORTANCE AND MEANING OF THE HARE KRISHNA MAHA-MANTRA
   The Significance of the Hare Krishna Maha-Mantra for This Present Age of Kali-yuga

CHAPTER FIVE: 43
THE MAHA-MANTRA IS THE BEST MEANS FOR SPIRITUAL REALIZATION
   Chanting the Maha-Mantra Purifies the Consciousness * Self-Realization Through Chanting * Important Benefits of Chanting the Holy Names * The Holy Name is Always Effective * Chanting the Holy Names is Best Process Even for Householders * Lord Vishnu's Names are More Powerful than the Greatest Holy Places

CHAPTER SIX: 68
THE GREAT GOOD FORTUNE OF ONE WHO CHANTS HARE KRISHNA
   The Bliss in Chanting the Holy Names * The Most Worshipful Object is the Holy Name

CHAPTER SEVEN: 76
ATTAINING LIBERATION THROUGH CHANTING
    How the Maha-Mantra can Deliver all Living Beings

CHAPTER EIGHT: 82
HOW TO CHANT THE HARE KRISHNA MAHA-MANTRA
    Putting it into Practice * Conclusion

CHAPTER NINE: 101
GOD INAUGURATES THE MAHA-MANTRA

CHAPTER TEN 108
THE HOLY NAME IS THE INCARNATION OF GOD FOR THE AGE OF KALI-YUGA

GLOSSARY 112

REFERENCES 122

INDEX 126

ABOUT THE AUTHOR 128

BOOKS BY STEPHEN KNAPP 131

CHAPTER ONE

Mantra-Yoga: A Necessity for this Age

Using mantras or prayers is a means of doing a number of things, depending on our purpose. First of all, it is a method to raise our consciousness and prepare ourselves for perceiving higher states of being. It can also help us enter into the spiritual dimension, or to invoke the blessings of the Divine. It is also a means to call on the positive energies to help us overcome obstacles, enemies, or to assist in healing our minds and bodies from disease or negativity. There are two basic kinds of mantras, those for spiritual and inner progress, and those for outer or more material needs. This little book is for only focusing on the means for spiritual progress, especially with the use of the Hare Krishna *maha-mantra*.

Concentrating on a mantra is also called mantra-yoga, especially when it is for our spiritual upliftment, or to unite us with the Supreme. Mantra-yoga, or the art of focusing on the sound vibrations in mantras or prayers, is actually a mystical tradition found in almost every spiritual path in the world. It may involve the softly spoken repetition of a prayer or mantra for one's own meditation, or it may be the congregational singing of spiritually uplifting songs, prayers, or sacred names of the Supreme Being. It all involves the same process, but in the Eastern tradition it is called mantra-yoga because it is the easy process of focusing our minds on the Supreme through His names, which helps spiritualize our consciousness. *Man* means the mind, *tra* means deliverance. Therefore, a spiritual mantra is the pure sound vibration for delivering the mind from material to spiritual consciousness. This is the goal of any spiritual path. Although all spiritual traditions have their own prayers or mantras, the Vedic Sanskrit mantras are especially powerful and effective in uniting us with the spiritual realm. However, a complete yoga process is generally a blend of a few yoga systems, such as ashtanga-yoga with bhakti-yoga, and bhakti-yoga with mantra-yoga. Therefore, some yoga systems also include mantra-yoga, or the process of concentrating on the sound vibration within a mantra. This is especially important in this age of Kali-yuga.

Many years ago the brahmana priests could accomplish many kinds of wondrous deeds simply by correctly chanting particular mantras. Many of these mantras still exist, but it is very difficult to find those who can chant them accurately. This is actually a safety measure because if the wish-fulfilling mantras were easily chanted, there would no doubt be many people who would misuse them. But other mantras that are available can easily help purify one's consciousness, give spiritual enlightenment, and put one in touch with the Supreme.

In *Bhagavad-gita* (10.25) Sri Krishna explains that He is the transcendental *om* mantra and that the chanting of *japa* (chanting a mantra quietly for one's own meditation) is the purest of His representations and sacrifices. It is understood that by chanting *japa* and hearing the holy sounds of the mantra, one can come to the platform of spiritual realization. This is the process of mantra-yoga. However, even though the mantra is powerful in itself, when the mantra is chanted by a great devotee, it becomes more powerful. This is also the effect when a disciple is fortunate enough to take initiation or *diksha* from a spiritually potent master who gives him a mantra for spiritual purposes. Then the disciple can make rapid progress by utilizing the mantra.

Sanskrit mantras often consist of eternal sound energies that have always existed, both within the universe as well as beyond it, and before its manifestation and after its annihilation. Such special mantras are part of the eternal sound vibration called *shabda-brahma*.

When it comes to mantras, the *Vedas* mention three types: *vedic*, *tantric* and *puranic*. These can be further divided into *sattvic*, *rajasic* and *tamasic*. The mantras that are *sattvic* or in the mode of goodness are chanted for light, wisdom, compassion, divine love, or God realization. They help bring peace, destroy karma, and bring one to perfection after death. The mantras that are *rajasic* or in the mode of passion are chanted for material benedictions, like blessings for a healthy child, prosperity, successful business, and so on. However, such mantras do not help one rise above karma, but force one to take rebirth in order to acquire the results of their karma. The mantras that are *tamasic* or in the mode of ignorance or darkness are also called "black magic." These are used for the deliberate manipulation of the material energy for one's own purpose. Thus, they are what could be called sinful, and are often used to call spirits or to assist one to perform deeds that may bring harm to others for one's own benefit.

Some mantras hold certain powers in their vibratory formulas that are directly related to particular Deities, divine personalities, or forms of God. In fact, they may represent the Deity in full. When they do, they are considered non-different from the Deity and the sound vibrations are spiritual in nature. The mantra can be a condensed form of spiritual energy of the Divinity. By the repetition of the mantra, the person who chants it invokes the energy and mercy of that Deity. Thus, the Deity reveals Himself or Herself to the *sadhaka*, who then overcomes illusion and realizes the spiritual position of the Deity and his or her relationship with the Deity. The six kinds of mantras used in this connection are:

1. Dhyana Mantras--mantras for meditation to mentally invoke the Deity's form, abode or pastimes.

2. Bija Mantras--the seed mantras or seed words that are used for meditation and purification of the articles used in

worship. Mantras often begin with these. They include such *bijas* or seed mantras as *Aim* and *Shrim*, which are often connected to the feminine or Devi. Or *Klim* which helps arouse the force of attraction to the object addressed in the mantra. Or *Krim* which is often connected to Kali or Devi, or *Gum* which is in association with Ganesh. The *bija* or seed mantras are derived from the 50 prime sounds which invoke various levels of energy and also the nature of the elements, such as water, air, earth, fire, etc., and are related to *om*.

3. Mula Mantras--root mantras are the essence of the Deity, used when offering certain articles during the worship to address the Lord or Deity.

4. Stutis and Stotras--mantras or prayers chanted before, during and after the worship to glorify the Lord's name, form, qualities, and pastimes.

5. Pranama Mantras--prayers offering obeisances to great personalities or to the Lord, often used at the end of worship.

6. Gayatri Mantras--Vedic or Pancharatrika mantras used to worship or invoke the blessings of the Divinity, or to focus the mind on God, and for invoking different moods, energies or powers.

The Vedic mantras, such as those coming from the four *samhitas* of the *Rig*, *Sama*, *Yajur*, and *Atharva Vedas*, are eternal or spiritual sound vibrations. They are not composed by any man at some particular point in history. They are part of the *shabda-brahma*, the eternal sound vibration. These mantras are like seeds of vast amounts of power and knowledge that are held within them. Thus, many scriptures explain that such powers cannot be fully revealed to someone unless such mantras have been received through the process of *diksha* or initiation from a spiritual master.

Besides this, the results of chanting a mantra depend on the chanter's conception or intent in the mind while chanting it. Thus, one must know the meaning or purpose of the mantra while reciting it. If one thinks the mantra is for attaining material goals, the person may get that. But if the inner purpose of the mantra is known to deliver one to the spiritual world, and a person chants it sincerely for that purpose, then that will be the reward rather than something minor or material, as long as the person does not prematurely give up chanting it.

Most Sanskrit mantras have several principles that you find in them. First, they are often handed down or revealed by sages or authorities who have attained self-realization by its use. They also generally use a particular meter or rhythm while chanting it. Plus, the mantra often represents a certain Deity. It also has a *bija* or seed word that gives it additional power, and the sound formula it contains has a special *shakti* or energy. And finally, constant repetition of the mantra will open or activate the key of it which then can reveal pure consciousness in the one who has been initiated into its use. The practice of repeating or chanting it for one's personal use is called *japa*. The *japa* or chanting it a required number of times is often what triggers its power within the consciousness of the chanter in which it reaches its *siddha*, or perfection and goal.

The mantra is thus a point of meditation for the mind, but also a formula or transcendental sound vibration, like the holy name of God, that releases its energy into one's consciousness. Thus it prepares one for perceiving higher states of reality. With constant practice of the appropriate mantra, and with the proper pronunciation and devotional mood, the mantra can reveal the Absolute Truth to the practitioner as well as one's own spiritual form and relationship that you may have with the Supreme Being.

This is why it is best that one should receive and be initiated into the chanting of the mantra by a qualified guru. Then the mantra will be especially effective and powerful, and carry special means of invoking realizations into the devotee who uses it.

Mantras can be divided into two additional categories, namely *saguna* and *nirguna*. *Saguna* mantras (those that describe personal traits) often are like prayers that invoke certain Deities or characteristics of the Absolute. *Nirguna* mantras (those that refer to the nature of the Absolute without qualities) describe the person's identification with the Absolute.

Mantras can be used in different ways. They can be chanted in whispers, or out loud, or silently within the mind. Generally each mantra has a recommendation as to which way works best. Some mantras, like the Hare Krishna mantra, can be used in any of these ways, as well as sung as a song with a group or congregation. Generally, this is done with a lead singer who sings the mantra in a particular melody, and then everyone else sings it afterwards. The more people who can follow it and join in, the more powerful the effect becomes.

Some mantras are meant to be chanted only within the mind because their vibration or wavelength is beyond ordinary sound. So the silent method helps invoke the energy within the consciousness. However, to first whisper it or softly speak the mantra correctly may help one be able to chant it silently and make a stronger connection with the mantra.

The repeated chanting of a mantra is called *japa*. It is explained in the Vedic texts that in this age of Kali-yuga the process of chanting *japa* or mantra meditation is much more effective than practicing other spiritual paths that include meditating on the void or Brahman effulgence, or trying to control the life air within the body as in raja-yoga. Plus, only a very few can become perfect at raising the *kundalini* force up through the various *chakras*, or moving the life air up to the top of the head for enlightenment, and then get it to leave the body at the right time to achieve full liberation. And meditating on the void becomes useless as soon as there is the slightest external distraction, which in this age of Kali-yuga is a continuous thing. Therefore, the most effective means of focusing the consciousness is to concentrate on the sound vibration of a mantra.

Using a mantra for *japa* meditation is a process to help rid ourselves of unwanted thoughts and to retain the one thought upon which we are concentrating. It helps us purify the mind of that which obstructs knowledge of our true self. As our concentration on the mantra frees our mind from random thoughts, and as the sound vibration of it raises the frequency level upon which we operate, our consciousness can become clear to observe our real nature.

In the word *japa*, the letter *"pa"* stands for that which removes or destroys all impurities and obstructions. The letter *"ja"* stands for that which puts an end to the cycle of birth and death. *Japa*, therefore, is a means of liberation when the proper mantra is used for destroying the mental impurities and negative and materialistic desires and impressions that exist in the mind and consciousness.

There are two mantras that are especially recommended in the Vedic literature to accomplish this. One is *omkara* or the *om* mantra, and the other is Hare Krishna, Hare Krishna, Krishna Krishna, Hare Hare/Hare Rama, Hare Rama, Rama Rama, Hare Hare, which is known as the *maha* or great mantra. It is explained that these two mantras can deliver one to the realm beyond material existence. But there are ways to use these mantras, which we will explain next.

CHAPTER TWO

The Om Mantra

Omkara (*pranava*) is considered to be the sound incarnation of the Supreme Personality of God and is identical with the Supreme Lord. It is one of the most important of all mantras, and is often used at the beginning of many of the Vedic mantras or *stotras* that we find. Thus, it is important to know its inner meaning and how it is meant to be pronounced.

Om is considered to be beginningless, changeless, supreme, and free from any external contamination. The *Narada-pancharatra* states: "When the transcendental sound vibration is practiced by a conditioned soul, the Supreme Lord is present on his tongue." The *Atharva-veda* and the *Mandukya Upanishad* both mention the importance of *omkara*. *Omkara* is said to be the beginning, middle and end, and is eternal, beyond all material restrictions or contaminations.

The *om* mantra is a most sacred syllable in Vedic culture. The *Vedas* glorify *om* as the origin of the *Vedas*, or the seed from which all of the *Vedas* grew. This is why *om* precedes every Vedic mantra. *Om* expands into the *vyahritis* (*bhuh, bhuvah* and *svaha*) that indicate the three planetary levels of the universe, or the whole creation. The *vyahritis* expand into the Brahma Gayatri mantra, and this expands into all of the Vedic literature.

Om is the sound substance of the Absolute, the seed of the universal manifestation, and connected to the infinite Brahman. It is a name of God. It is also composed of the letters A, U and M, AUM. Several meanings for these have been written in the Sanskrit texts. "A" represents that which is observed in the state of wakefulness, or the experience of the body and senses. "U" represents that which is observed in the dream state, or the inner astral realm. "M" represents that which is in the state of deep sleep as well as that which is beyond the perception of the senses in the wakeful state. The silence, which is like the fourth letter of AUM, is the basis and underlying reality found in all states of consciousness, whether waking, dreaming or deep sleep. This is the Brahman, which is all that is manifested and all that is unmanifest.

It is also said by some that the letters of AUM represent Brahma, Vishnu and Shiva, or the principles of universal creation, maintenance and destruction. The idea is that the vibration of AUM was the initial cause that lead to the creation, and continues the cycles of maintenance and destruction of the universe.

However, *om* also reveals itself according to the depth of consciousness and realizations of the practitioner or *sadhaka*. For example, it is also described by the Gosvamis of Vrindavana that, on a different level, the letter A (*a-kara*) refers to the Supreme Being, Krishna, the master of all living beings and all material and spiritual worlds. He is the Supreme Leader. The letter U (*u-kara*) represents Radharani, or the pleasure potency or spiritual energy of the Supreme, otherwise known as the feminine aspect of God. The M (*ma-kara*) represents the living beings, the marginal energy of the Supreme. Thus, *om* is the complete combination of the Absolute Truth. In other words, *omkara* represents the Supreme Being, His name (Krishna), fame, pastimes, entourage, expansions, energies, and everything else. Thus, *om* is also the resting place of everything and the full understanding of the *Vedas* and all Vedic knowledge.

Further information relates that *omkara*, as the representation of the Supreme Lord, delivers one back to the spiritual dimension if one remembers or chants it at the time of death. Srila Jiva Gosvami, in his *Bhagavat-sandarbha*, says that *omkara* is considered the sound vibration of the holy name of the Supreme Lord. The *Srimad-Bhagavatam* also begins with *omkara*. Thus it is considered the seed of deliverance from the material world. Since the Supreme is absolute, then both He and His name are the same. Contact with the name is also contact with the Lord Himself.

In the *Srimad-Bhagavatam* (12.6.37-49) we find Suta Goswami describe how the *Om* came into existence and was the basis of the expansion of the Vedic literature. He explains, "O brahmana, first the subtle vibration of transcendental sound appeared from the sky of the heart of the most elevated Lord Brahma, whose mind was perfectly fixed in spiritual realization. One can perceive this subtle vibration when one stops all external hearing. By worship of this subtle form of the *Vedas*, O brahmana, mystic sages cleanse their hearts of all contamination caused by impurity of substance, activity and doer, and thus they attain freedom from repeated birth and death. From that transcendental subtle vibration arose the *omkara* composed of three sounds. The *omkara* has unseen potencies and manifests automatically within a purified heart. It is the representation of the Absolute Truth in all three of His phases--the Supreme Personality, the Supreme Soul, and the supreme impersonal truth.

"This *omkara*, ultimately nonmaterial and imperceptible, is heard by the Supersoul without His possessing material ears or any other material senses. The entire expanse of Vedic sound is elaborated from *omkara*, which appears from the soul, within the sky of the heart. It is the direct designation of the self-originating Absolute Truth, the Supersoul, and is the secret essence and eternal seed of all Vedic hymns. *Omkara* exhibited the three original sounds of the alphabet--A, U, and M. These three, O most eminent descendant of Bhrigu, sustain all the different threefold aspects of material existence, including the three modes of nature, the name of the *Rig*, *Yajur* and *Sama Vedas*, the goals of the Bhur, Bhuvar and Svar planetary systems, and the three

Chapter Two 13

functional platforms called waking consciousness, sleep and deep sleep.

"From *omkara* Lord Brahma created all the sounds of the alphabet--the vowels, consonants, semivowels, sibilants, and others--distinguished by such features as long and short measure. All-powerful Brahma made use of this collection of sounds to produce from his four faces the four *Vedas*, which appeared together with the sacred *omkara* and the seven *vyahriti* invocations. His intention was to propagate the process of Vedic sacrifice according to the different functions performed by the priests of each of the four *Vedas*. Brahma taught these Vedas to his sons, who were great sages among the brahmanas and experts in the art of Vedic recitation. They in turn took the role of *acharyas* and imparted the *Vedas* to their own sons.

"In this way, throughout the cycles of four ages [*yugas*], generation after generation of disciples--all firmly fixed in their spiritual vows--have received these *Vedas* by disciplic succession. At the end of each Dvapara-yuga the *Vedas* are edited into separate divisions by eminent sages. Observing that people in general were diminished in their life span, strength and intelligence by the influence of time, great sages took inspiration from the Personality of Godhead sitting within their hearts and systematically divided the *Vedas*. O brahmana, in the present age of Vaivasvata Manu, the leaders of the universe, led by Brahma and Shiva, requested the Supreme Personality of Godhead, the protector of all the worlds, to save the principles of religion. O most fortunate Shaunaka, the almighty Lord, exhibiting a divine spark of a portion of His plenary portion, then appeared in the womb of Satyavati as the son of Parashara. In this form, named Krishna Dvaipayana Vyasa [Vyasadeva], he divided the one *Veda* into four."

Herein we can understand how the *Om* was manifested and how the transcendental knowledge that was incorporated in it was the foundation that was expanded into the many Vedic texts that we have today. From the four *Vedas* followed by the *Upanishads*, *Vedanta Sutras*, the *Itihasas* like the *Ramayana* and *Mahabharata*, and on to the *Puranas*, with many others along the way.

The image of *om* looks something like the number 3 with an extra curve. The largest lower curve represents the waking state. The upper curve signifies deep dreamless sleep. The additional lower curve is the dream state. [Some say the large lower curve is the dream state, the upper curve is the waking state, and the side lower curve is the deep dreamless sleep.] The dot represents the Absolute Reality which is separated from the other curves (or states of consciousness) by a half-circle. This half-circle signifies *maya*, the illusion or material energy which separates the Absolute Reality from the different levels of material consciousness. It is *maya* which keeps us focused on various states of consciousness within the realm of the material manifestation which then veils the Absolute from our experience or awareness. The half-circle, being open on top, indicates the infinite and unbounded nature of the Absolute, which is always separate from *maya*.

Om, therefore, is the summation of the indescribable reality. It is the encapsulated form of all that is. When AUM is pronounced properly, the "A" begins from the base of the spine, the Muladhara Chakra. As the sound moves up, the "A" or *A-kara* activates the area of the naval and the digestive system.

The "U" sound comes from the heart area, so our blood circulation becomes activated. The heart gets the extra supply of oxygen, which then spreads through other parts of the body. The sound of "U" is pronounced in the throat region, ending at the tongue's tip. The "M" is focused at the lips, or the end of the vocal mechanism. It goes in our head and comes out through our nose, which stimulates the vibrations in the brain. This also helps activate the pituitary gland and helps the over-all improvement of the body. Plus the psychic abilities are awakened. Thus, when *om* is chanted or pronounced correctly, it includes all the sounds or vowels of the alphabet.

In the last part of the mantra is the silence into which the *om* culminates. It is the *om* without the distinction of parts. It has no name and thus does not come under the purview of empirical usage. It is the self or pure consciousness, the *turiya*, which transcends all distinctions.

Om is also said to be the sound of the universe, or the sound of the energy which flows through it. Thus, to meditate on *om* in deep attention leads one's mind into profound states of higher consciousness. *Omkara* is unlimited, transcendental, and indestructible. As such, it is not so easy for the average person to understand all the intricacies of *om* or to chant it properly, and, thus, reach the *siddha* or perfection by chanting it.

It is said that additional benefits of chanting *Om* properly include gaining strength and stability of the mind; filling the mind with light; brings about creative will, wisdom and right action; eliminates stress, anxiety and depression; stimulates the brain; enhances the ability to focus the mind; brings in superior thoughts; brings in higher vibrations which effects the body, mind and organs in a positive way; improves memory and concentration, among other things.

Actually, the chanting of *omkara* is generally practiced by those engaged in the mystic yoga process. However, anyone who chants Vedic verses will also be chanting *om*, because *om* is often included as a *bija* or seed mantra at the beginning of many such verses or mantras. By chanting *om* and controlling the breathing perfectly, which is mostly a mechanical way of steadying the mind, one is eventually able to go into trance or *samadhi*. Through this system, one gradually changes the tendencies of the materially absorbed mind and makes it spiritualized. But this takes many years to perfect and such a slow process is hardly practical in this age for the average person. If one is not initiated into the brahminical way of knowledge, he will find it difficult to understand the depths of *omkara* and will not likely be able to get the desired results from chanting it. Therefore, it is not advised that people in general chant *omkara* in this age of Kali-yuga with the expectation of using it to reach full spiritual perfection because they are often not qualified or unable to chant it properly to attain the inner depths of spiritual completion. But there is no harm in trying or in using it, as there are no adverse effects as with some mantras.

OM MEDITATION TECHNIQUE

The correct procedure for chanting *om* is as follows:
1. Sit in your meditation posture with eyes closed and your mind at peace. The head, neck and spine must be straight. Prepare yourself appropriately with relaxation, deep breathing and *pranayama*,
2. When ready, take in a deep breath slowly until it reaches the naval, hold it comfortably,
3. Then begin to utter *om* with a long exhale, going ooooooommmmm or aaaaauuuuummmmm. You first chant the "A" or "aaahhh" sound during the main portion of the exhale, and then go to pronouncing the "U" or "uh" sound,

and conclude with the "M" sound. The "A" is chanted through parted lips, slowly ascending in volume. The "U" is chanted through lips that are closer together. The time taken for chanting the "U" should be double the time taken for chanting "A". The last sound "M" is uttered through the nose with lips closed. The time for chanting "M" should be double that for "U". As you chant the "M" the volume of the sound should descend as slowly as it rose during the "A", taking as much time as it took to ascend.

4. Chant it like this several times for a total of at least nine times.

5. As you chant, do it more quietly until it is a whisper, bringing your awareness deeper within yourself each time.

6. Then chant even more deeply, but only mentally, not out loud. Let the sound pervade and resonate in your mind. It should be the only thing that you hear.

7. The next step is when this form of meditation gets more difficult. Now cease the mental chanting while still listening to the sound within your awareness. Let yourself flow into that sound, losing all other identity and all other awareness. Nothing else exists. Only you and *om*, the vibration of God. Your focus on it should be steady and without effort, as if you are simply flowing with it. Within that vibration is all there is. If you can reach this level of awareness, then for several minutes or as long as you can, if you are aware of time at all, sit in that awareness of God, the Absolute, the Pure, the Omniscient and Supreme Being. Let that awareness fill your being completely, and thus make you complete as part of the Complete Whole.

Herein you may begin to see that to really reach the full perfection of this form of meditation is not so easy for most people. This is why some sages feel, and some references in *shastra* state, that this can be a nice preliminary form of practice, but should not be expected to take people to the deepest level of realization simply because most people in the age of Kali-yuga will find it too difficult. There are simply too many distractions to reach the desired success with it, especially for step number seven, and the mental strength and concentration needed are rarely to be found these days. Nonetheless, people can still use it as best they can, and different results will be determined by the particular consciousness of each individual.

The mantra that is especially meant to be chanted in this age is easy and actually more directly connected with the Supreme than the sound vibration of *omkara* because it contains the holy names and the same spiritual energy of the Lord. It can be used in any number of ways to help focus the minds of people on all levels of awareness. This mantra for Kali-yuga is the *maha-mantra*, also called the great mantra for deliverance, which is Hare Krishna, Hare Krishna, Krishna Krishna, Hare Hare/Hare Rama, Hare Rama, Rama Rama, Hare Hare.

CHAPTER THREE

The Power of the Maha-Mantra: How it Works

It may be somewhat surprising for the average Westerner to hear about the power within the vibrations of words or mantras, but the potency is real. For example, any numerologist will tell you that each letter has a particular value and a group of letters pronounced as a word invokes the power of those letters. Therefore, someone's name contains the subtle formula for signifying to varying degrees one's characteristics, qualities and future. By associating with particular sound vibrations one becomes influenced by them.

A good example of this is when one country tries to take over another in war, or one political party tries to defeat another. The first thing they try to do is take over the lines of communication and the media, such as radio, television and newspapers. By sending out its propaganda through sound, a government can influence people's minds and stay in power, or a political party can remove the leaders of the opposition. In the latter case, a new government may become established.

According to the predominant types of sound vibration people associate with through T.V. and radio, or in reading articles in magazines and newspapers, they become attracted to certain things or drawn towards certain viewpoints. When television shows, songs on the radio, stories in magazines, and advertising everywhere propagates the concern for temporary sense gratification, then people lose their interest in the real goal of life. They simply become absorbed in the thoughts of whatever type of sound vibration enters their consciousness. When nonsensical sound vibrations enter and contaminate the ether, the air, water, and the very molecular structure of each and every person, place and thing, then we cannot expect anything else but continued and worsening turmoil and perplexities in the world.

Let us try to understand how this happens. First of all, energy pervades the atmosphere of this creation in the form of vibrations, as in sound waves, light waves, radio waves, and so on. The mind can especially be affected by the kind of energy or vibration it picks up or tunes into. The function of the mind is twofold: it joins thoughts and concepts into theories and goals or desires, and it simplifies or interprets experiences that are gathered through the senses. This is controlled by sound vibration or thought waves. For example, when you hear the following words, an image will form in your mind: dog, cat, insect, man, woman, politician, automobile, and sunset. We can take the experiment a little further when we say, snarling dog, sleeping cat, biting insect, ugly old man, beautiful voluptuous woman, conniving politician, sleek automobile, and tranquil red sunset.

The second set of words may have brought images to your mind that were completely different than the first set. This is all due to sound which triggers the mind to react and form thoughts or images related to the words by interpreting past experiences. Such thoughts and images may also form into goals or desires of what we want to attain or wish to avoid. When throughout our life we are bombarded by different kinds of sound waves, whether from schoolbooks in our early years, or to present-day radio, television, and movies, our consciousness is led through particular changes and different levels of development. This might be controlled by others so that we act in a certain way according to someone else's design, whether we know it or not. If you start listening to the radio all the time and all they play are songs about making love under the apple tree, you will not have to tell anyone what you will be thinking about. It is not difficult to figure out. This is how we are controlled by sound.

Another example is that sometime we may be feeling peaceful and decide to spend a nice, quiet evening watching television. After several hours of being exposed to all kinds of sound vibration in the form of game shows, cop shows, comedy, soap opera, news, and a multitude of advertising, we may wake up the next morning unrested, agitated, and disturbed without knowing why. But the kind of energy we imbibed through sound will continue to have an affect on us later. In this way, the kind of sound vibration we associate with can make a big difference on our consciousness.

There are, however, many kinds of beneficial sound vibrations that we can utilize. A friend of mine once cut his finger down to the bone while he was in India. It was a serious cut and he was not able to do much to stop the bleeding. He told one of the Indian men nearby who took him into his house. The man put some mustard seed oil on the cut and stroked it with his finger while chanting a certain mantra. At that point the bleeding stopped. He did it again and the cut closed. The man did it a third time and, to my friend's amazement, the cut on his finger was practically healed. Some farmers also use mantras to produce better crops. Plants are very sensitive to vibrations and different sounds can assist plants in their growth.

In the Vedic literature there are, of course, many stories that describe the use of mantras. The brahmana priests produced many kinds of magical results by using them. They could even curse others or, if necessary, kill someone with the use of mantras. The warriors or kings could also attach a *brahmastra* weapon to the arrows they shot. A *brahmastra* is a weapon equivalent to the atomic bombs of today, but were produced by perfectly chanting particular mantras. However, the *brahmastra* could also be called back by using a different mantra and the extent of damage could also be controlled. They were not like the bombs of today that, when released, are completely uncontrollable and kill and hurt everyone and anyone in its range.

There are many other kinds of sound vibrations, mantras, or prayers that can be used for gaining money, maintaining health, defeating enemies, getting good luck, subduing evil spirits, counteracting snake bite, and so on. There are countless mantras or prayers for temporary results, not only in the Vedic culture but in other cultures as well. The most powerful mantras are those that can completely free one from this material world and the cycle of birth and death and allow one to enter the spiritual realm. As already established, there is no mantra more powerful for this purpose than the Hare Krishna *maha-mantra*.

The way the *maha-mantra* works is a science. One thing we must first understand is that there are channels by which the Infinite descends into this world. One channel is through transcendental sound. The *maha-mantra* is a purely spiritual vibration. It cannot be chanted with a material tongue nor heard with a material ear. In this way, the holy name reserves the right of not being exposed to organic senses or understood by someone in materialistic consciousness. However, the Infinite has the power of making Himself known to the finite mind. When He reveals Himself to His devotee, the devotee experiences the perception of God. This is called Self-realization and transcendental revelation. This can be attained through the process of purely chanting the *maha-mantra*.

The holy names are not revealed simply through Vedic writings, but they are revealed to the world through the spiritual tongues of the pure devotees. Such pure devotees are the real spiritual masters of everyone in the universe. But if the guru is not genuine, then the sound or mantra, though seeming to sound the same, will not produce the real effect.

Chapter Three

The audience of the pure devotee hears the name of Krishna but may not fully recognize or comprehend it. Yet the name enters the ear and vibrates the eardrum which touches our mind. There is still not genuine spiritual realization at this point because the soul remains untouched. Yet the name begins to affect our mind by cleansing the dust within. This dust is the materialistic consciousness that causes forgetfulness of our real spiritual identity. This forgetfulness manifests in forms of bodily attachment, lust, greed, envy, anger, etc. Therefore, by chanting the *maha-mantra* we wash our mind and enable it to get free of the contaminating dust. Then the mind and intelligence become very clear and sharp. Plus when the Supersoul hears our sincere attempt to chant the holy names, He will also assist us in clearing away any obstacles in our path. Thus, our ability increases to delve more deeply into spiritual understanding and to acquire a taste for the holy names.

The mind is the connecting link between the body and the spirit soul within. The soul, which does not actively engage in any material activities, remains in a state of suspended animation while covered by illusion, as in the case of a materially conditioned person who engages in material activities. Through the vehicle of the mind, the senses act and we perceive things around us and form theories. If the mind is unclear or dusty due to the influence of the material energy, we then become confused about the goal of life and may engage in so many material pursuits. When the mind is cleansed or purified by associating with the Infinite in the form of the *maha-mantra*, all our material concoctions are forced out. By inundating our mind with the transcendental sound of the holy names, all of our misconceptions, which is the cause of our material suffering, are completely conquered, leaving no more enemies within the mind. Then the mind reflects the quality and nature of the soul.

The holy sound of Hare Krishna, as uttered by the pure devotee, moves our intellect and we begin to consider the

Vedic philosophy. When the intelligence is thus energized by spiritual knowledge, the transcendental sound vibration, after cutting through the senses, mind, and intelligence, makes contact with the soul. Thus, we are able to hear the holy name with our real spiritual ear, and actual spiritual revelation and Self-realization is open to us. Then the soul, having made contact with the Supreme or Supersoul through the form of transcendental sound, recapitulates, sending the vibration back through our intelligence, mind and senses. At that time, when we chant Hare Krishna, the Supreme Infinite Lord is there in the vibration and our whole being experiences a deluge of unlimited spiritual ecstasy.

From this level of spiritual realization, we can enter into the understanding of the very cause of everything that exists. The mind, body, and soul, and even material nature itself can be changed into transcendental energy by one pure exclamation of Hare Krishna. This is very important to understand because when everything becomes saturated with this transcendental sound, the result is total transformation of energy. Thus, what is material can be changed into something spiritual. If this can be done on a grand scale, the material world can be transformed into the spiritual world.

Another example of how the holy names of Krishna work, and how powerful they are, can be cited from the *Srimad-Bhagavatam*, Sixth Canto, in the story of Ajamila. Ajamila was born of good parents who trained him in knowledge of the *Vedas* to become a perfect brahmana. Yet one time, while walking along the road, he happened to see a man and a prostitute in a state of intoxication, frolicking in the grass. The woman was not covered properly and was uninhibitedly engaging in amorous pastimes with the man. Upon seeing this, Ajamila became very agitated and later sought the company of the prostitute. He left his young beautiful wife and lived with the prostitute, giving up all regulative principles. He begot ten sons in the womb of the

Chapter Three

prostitute and named the youngest son Narayana, a name of one of the expansions of Krishna.

To maintain himself and his family, Ajamila cheated others in gambling or by robbing them. While he spent his time in abominable, sinful activities, eighty-eight years of his life passed by. Since his youngest son was born while Ajamila was very old, Narayana was very dear to him. Because of the child's awkward manners and speech, Ajamila delighted in the child's activities. When Ajamila ate or drank, he always did so with his son, Narayana. Ajamila, however, could not understand that the length of his life was decreasing and death was approaching. When the time of death arrived for Ajamila, he began to think only of his son.

At the moment of death, Ajamila became extremely frightened when he saw three persons with deformed bodies, fierce, twisted faces, and their hair standing erect. These were the Yamadutas, the soldiers of Yamaraja, the lord of death. With a noose in their hands, they had come to take him to Yamaraja. Because of attachment to his son, Ajamila fearfully began to call him loudly by his name, Narayana.

Just then the Vishnudutas, soldiers of Lord Vishnu, arrived when they heard the holy name of their master from the mouth of the dying Ajamila. Ajamila had certainly chanted the name of Narayana without offense because he had chanted in complete anxiety. The Yamadutas were snatching the soul from the heart of Ajamila, but the messengers of Lord Vishnu forcefully stopped them from doing so. The Yamadutas inquired why they were being stopped from taking Ajamila. The Vishnudutas then asked the Yamadutas that if they were really servants of Lord Yamaraja, then explain the meaning of religious and irreligious principles.

The Yamadutas replied that from their master, Yamaraja, they had heard that which is prescribed in the *Vedas* constitutes religious principles, and the opposite is irreligion. They continued to explain that Lord Narayana is situated in His own abode in the spiritual world, but controls the entire cosmic creation. The sun, fire, sky, air, demigods, moon, evening, day, night, directions, water, land, and Supersoul Himself all witness the activities of the living entities. Those that deserve punishment are those who are confirmed by these witnesses as having engaged in unrighteous activities. Everyone engaged in fruitive activities deserves punishment in proportion to their sinful acts. In this way, they must enjoy or suffer the corresponding reactions of their karma in the next life.

The Yamadutas continued to explain the laws of karma and the position of the living entity, pointing out that in considering the sinful life of Ajamila, they had the right to take him to hell in order to rectify his sinful behavior.

The Vishnudutas, however, stated that Ajamila had already atoned for all of his sinful actions, not only for this one life but for those performed in millions of lives, simply by chanting the holy name of Narayana in a helpless condition. Even though he had not chanted purely, he chanted without offense, and, therefore, was now pure and eligible for liberation. Throughout Ajamila's life, he called the name Narayana. Although calling his son, by chanting the name Narayana, he sufficiently atoned for the sinful actions of millions of lives. At the time of death, Ajamila had helplessly and very loudly chanted the holy name of the Lord. That chanting alone had already freed him from the reactions of all sinful life. Therefore, the soldiers of Lord Vishnu forbade the servants of Yamaraja to take Ajamila for punishment in hell. Anyone who takes shelter of the Supreme through His holy names can similarly be saved from the dark future of sinful reactions after death.

Although *Srimad-Bhagavatam* relates the full story of Ajamila and how he witnessed the discussion between the Yamadutas and Vishnudutas and then went on to achieve ultimate spiritual perfection by taking to the process of bhakti-yoga, our short summary here is to show the potency of the holy names. Ajamila is not much different than most people in this age of Kali who are attracted to sinful activities. Therefore, we should seriously try to understand and take advantage of the chanting of the holy names, for by doing so even the greatest sins we may have committed can be atoned, as the following verses explain:

> Simply by chanting one holy name of Hari, a sinful man can counteract the reactions to more sins than he can commit. (*Brihad-vishnu Purana*)
>
> As when all small animals flee in fear when a lion roars, similarly all one's sinful reactions leave when a person chants the Lord's holy names while in a helpless condition or even if he has no desire to do so. (*Garuda Purana*)
>
> The path to liberation is guaranteed when a person once chants the holy name of Lord Hari. (*Skanda Purana*)

The *Srimad-Bhagavatam* (6.3.31) explains that chanting the holy names can negate the reactions of the most serious of sins, and, therefore, everyone should take this seriously and join the *sankirtana* movement (the movement for congregational chanting of the holy names of Krishna), which is the most auspicious activity in the universe. And the *Caitanya-caritamrita* (Madhya-lila, 15.109) discloses that beyond dissolving one's entanglement in material existence, by chanting Krishna's names one develops attraction and awakens his love for Krishna.

From these verses we can understand that there is no impediment for everyone to readily utilize the holy names to purify themselves of even the worst sins, providing they are sincere and chant purely. Even those who cannot speak properly can repeat the *maha-mantra* within their minds.

From those who are the most saintly to those who are in the most abominable position, all have the opportunity of chanting the holy names to begin the escape from karmic reactions and to free themselves from material entanglement. As described in *Srimad-Bhagavatam* (6.2.9-10), the chanting of the names of the Supreme is the best atonement for one who is a thief, a drunkard, a killer of *brahmanas*, or one who kills women or kings or cows or his own parents, or for any other kind of sins. Simply by chanting the holy names one attracts the attention of the Supreme who gives that person special protection.

Herein we can discern that attracting the attention of the Supreme by chanting His holy names is the best means of protecting ourselves from our past impurities. This does not mean we can continue doing such sinful acts, but when we have stopped them and felt remorse, then we can engage in sincere chanting of the Lord's holy names. When the Supreme is pleased with someone, what can they not accomplish? Anything can be done by one who becomes spiritually powerful. Therefore, out of all the various processes of atonement that are prescribed by different scripture, engaging in the chanting of the holy names is best because it actually uproots the material desires in the heart. As the *Bhagavatam* (6.2.12) confirms, the various processes of atonement are not complete if one's mind still runs back to unwanted material habits. Therefore, those who want freedom from their karmic reactions, chanting of the names and pastimes of the Supreme is the best because it completely purifies the mind.

It further relates that chanting the holy names of the Lord before dying by some misfortune is enough to deliver a person from having to enter hell to suffer for his bad karmic reactions. (*Srimad-Bhagavatam* 6.2.15)

Not only is the name of the Lord so powerfully effective on one who seriously chants it, despite the fact that he may have been sinful in his past, the name also acts on one who chants it in a very casual manner. The *Bhagavatam* points out that even if one chants the holy names neglectfully, jokingly, or simply for entertainment, the holy names are nonetheless effective enough to free the person from unlimited sins, just as a powerful medicine is effective whether a patient who takes it understands it or not. (*Bhag.* 6.2.14, 19)

Even making an offense to God Himself or to the holy names, such offenses can be mitigated by taking shelter of chanting the Lord's holy names. This is related in the *Padma Purana* (4.25.22-27) as follows: When somehow a sin or blemish is committed against the name of Vishnu, the person should always recite the name and sincerely seek its refuge only. Lord Vishnu's names alone remove the sin of those who have committed a sin or offence against the names since they alone, continuously recited, bring wealth. It is the name alone, when recited without interruption, when remembered or heard, either in a pure form or with incorrect syllables, would protect a man. This alone is the truth. Of course, if it is resorted to hypocritically or for greed born of love for body or wealth, it would not quickly produce the desired result. O Narada, this great secret, which removes all inauspiciousness, and keeps off all sins, was formerly heard (by me) from Shiva. O Narada, even those who are intent on committing sins [but refrain from such], but who know the names of Vishnu would be liberated merely by reciting them.

Pondering all these points, Lord Yamaraja, in the *Srimad-Bhagavatam* (6.3.26), concludes that all intelligent men take to devotional service by chanting the holy names of the Supreme because even if they accidentally perform some sinful act, they are protected since the chanting of the Hare Krishna mantra obliterates all sinful reactions.

Besides this, the *maha-mantra* purifies our consciousness to reveal our spiritual identity and our connection with the Supreme. In this way, the *maha-mantra* accomplishes all necessities on our spiritual path.

CHAPTER FOUR

The Importance and Meaning of The Hare Krishna Maha-Mantra

One of the most important principles in the process of bhakti-yoga is the chanting of the holy names of the Lord, especially in the form of the Hare Krishna *maha-mantra*. The word *maha* means "great," as in the greatest mantra for deliverance. This means delivering the mind from unnecessary thoughts, agitation, worries, and concerns, and to bring the spiritual vibration into our consciousness. Furthermore, this mantra can be chanted quietly for personal development as in *japa* meditation, as when we chant it a certain number of times on beads, or it can be sung in a group as in congregational chanting or singing, called *sankirtan*. It also has numerous melodies that can be used along with instruments to inspire and enthuse everyone who wants to chant or sing along.

Even in the early Vedic literature of the *Rig Veda* (1.156.3) we find the following prayers that describe many of the unique characteristics and potencies of the name of God, in this case in the name of Vishnu: "O Supreme Lord, Sri Vishnu! Your sacred *nama* [name] is absolutely cognizant and all-illuminating because the entire Vedic scripture have emanated from You. Your name is the wellspring of supreme

Chapter Four

bliss, the embodiment of Brahman, is readily available, and is full of transcendental knowledge. We meditate upon the purport of Your name, discuss [Your] name amongst ourselves, and chant Your name continuously. In this way, we worship You.

"O Sri Vishnu, ever since our faith in You has become steadfast, our desire to gain Your direct audience has led us to offer incessant prayers at Your lotus feet, which are the purifying agents of the hearts of the devotees and replete with relishable transcendental pastimes. We always hear the glorification of Your unsurpassable qualities and praise them amongst ourselves. In this way, we have taken shelter of Your omnipotent and all-purifying name.

"O sages. Know for certain that the original primeval Supreme Personality of Godhead you seek is Sri Krishna. Worship Him in this realization, for He is the ultimate goal of the Vedas, the absolute essence. He is the embodiment of eternity, absolute knowledge, and divine bliss. The purpose of human life is to know Him, to describe Him and the wonderful pastimes of His incarnations. Let us eulogize and worship that Supreme Lord according to our natural spiritual emotions and taste. In this way, we shall crown our lives with paramount success and continuously chant *harinama* [the names of Hari, Lord Krishna who takes away all inauspiciousness], which is dynamic, variegated and omnipotent. To chant *harinama* is the most relishable activity, and the bestower of the greatest pleasure."

This description certainly gives great insight into the potencies of the holy names and how to unleash those potencies by the most blissful activity of discussing the nature of the Lord and to engage in the congregational chanting of the holy names, which is called *harinama sankirtana*.

To understand deeper meanings and significance of the name Krishna, or any of His holy names, we need to first accept the premise that the name of Krishna and Krishna Himself are composed of the same spiritual energy. There is no difference. All words have significance, but if I chant the name of water, I do not get the experience of water. My thirst remains unquenched. The point is that we can experience the presence of Krishna just by sincerely chanting His name with faith and devotion. It will begin to reveal itself to us, and we can actually have the experience of Krishna's presence if we treat the name with the respect that it is due.

This is explained like so, "The Lord's holy name, His form and personality are all one and the same. There is no difference between them. Since all of them are absolute, they are transcendentally blissful. There is no difference between Krishna's body and Himself or between His name and Himself. As far as the conditioned soul is concerned, everything is difference. One's name is different from the body, from one's original form and so on." (*Caitanya-caritamrta*, Madhya-lila, 17. 131-2)

"The holy name of Krishna, His transcendental qualities and pastimes as well as Lord Krishna Himself are all equal. They are all spiritual and full of bliss." (*Cc.* Madhya, 17.135)

Another example is from the *Padma Purana*, as quoted in the *Caitanya-caritamrita* (Madhya.17.133), which explains it this way, "The sacred name of Krishna is transcendentally blissful. It bestows all spiritual benedictions, for it is Krishna Himself, the reservoir of all pleasure. Krishna's name is complete, and it is the form of all transcendental mellows. It is not a material name under any condition, and it is no less powerful than Krishna Himself. Since Krishna's name is not contaminated by the material qualities, there is no question of its being involved with *maya* [the temporary material energy]. The name of Krishna is always liberated and spiritual; it is never conditioned by the laws of material nature. This is because the name of Krishna and Krishna Himself are identical."

Chapter Four

In the *Agni Purana* it is said, "Whoever chants the words 'Hare Krishna, Hare Krishna, Krishna Krishna, Hare Hare' even negligently will achieve the goal, without doubt."

Then in the *Brahmanda Purana* it is also said, "Whoever chants 'Hare Rama, Hare Rama, Rama Rama, Hare Hare,' is freed from all sins."

It was Sri Chaitanya Mahaprabhu, the greatest preacher of the glories of the holy name, who combined these two statements, thereby issuing the words Hare Krishna and Hare Rama to drown the world in love of God, Krishna *prema*. Even though this mantra had been described previously in Vedic literature, Sri Chaitanya Mahaprabhu taught His followers and the world to chant the sixteen-word mantra, Hare Krishna, Hare Krishna, Krishna Krishna, Hare Hare / Hare Rama, Hare Rama, Rama Rama, Hare Hare.

The mystery behind these names of God is further explained in the *Sri Caitanya Upanishad*, texts 12-14. It explains that the names of the Supreme that are used in the Hare Krishna mantra have specific meanings. *Hari* refers to "He who unties the knot of a person's material desires." Krishna is divided into *Krish*, which means "He who is attractive to everyone," and *Na*, which means "the greatest spiritual pleasure." And *Rama* means "He who is full of spiritual bliss and attracts all others." The Hare Krishna mantra consists of the repetition of these names of the Supreme (Hare Krishna, Hare Krishna, Krishna Krishna, Hare Hare / Hare Rama, Hare Rama, Rama Rama, Hare Hare) and is the best of all mantras and most confidential of secrets. Those who are serious about making spiritual progress continually chant these holy names and cross over material existence.

This is also elaborated in the *Agamas* and the *Gautamiya Tantra*, which describe that the root '*krs*' means 'to attract' and the suffix '*na*' means 'ultimate bliss.' Together these two roots form the word *Krishna*, which means the person who attracts, and the personification of the ultimate bliss. This is the Supreme Brahman or ultimate Supreme Being. So it would seem natural that if we are going to work for anything, why not simply work for the ultimate bliss? The *Agamas* further explain that by uttering the syllable '*ra*', all sins are driven away. But in order to keep them from returning, the syllable '*ma*' is added, as if in closing the door. Also in the *Ramatapini Upanishad* the person who enjoys with Radha is called Rama. This refers to Krishna, who gives pleasure to the yogis, meaning the bhakti-yogis or devotees. (*Sri Caitanya-Siksamrita*, p.227-8)

There is still another point of significance to these names. The *Padma Purana* also explains that Rama means the all-conscious and all-blissful Divinity who permeates the whole world, and in whom the yogis find joy. The *Mahabharata* (Udyoga Parva, 70.5) also says that the syllable '*krs*' means existence, and '*na*' means joy or bliss. Thus the name Krishna also means the everlasting, immortal and eternal joy. Then the word *Hari* means one who takes away all sins or all inauspiciousness, and who burns all the sins of one who recites His name.

The Hare Krishna mantra also directs one's attention and devotion to Radha as well as Krishna. Radha is also known as Mother Hara, which is the name Hare in the vocative form within the mantra. So in chanting Hare Krishna, we are first approaching the Lord's internal potency and asking Radha to please engage us in the service of Lord Krishna. Concentrating on Krishna through His names is one form of that service. In other words, it is through Radha that one more easily attains Krishna and service to Krishna. This is the advantage of approaching Lord Krishna through Radharani as in the Hare Krishna mantra.

Therefore, while chanting this Hare Krishna mantra in *japa* [personal meditation] or *sankirtana* [congregational chanting or singing], the *sadhaka* or practitioner should dwell on the meaning of these divine names, and should believe that the all-pervading Supreme Being has appeared before him in the form of the holy name. Thinking like this and to consider the unfathomable opportunity a person has because of being introduced to the Lord in His name, gives increasing joy and peace of mind. In this way, the *sadhaka* can keep his mind fixed on the Divine Form of the Lord as his *Ishta-devata*, his chosen Divinity.

It is also through this name that Krishna calls out to all of His eternal servants, both devotees and the materially conditioned souls, like a cow who has lost her calf. He scatters His name amongst them through the mercy of the pure devotees who spread these holy names in hope that people everywhere will get a glimpse of the supreme bliss that is available if they would only decrease their material attractions and look within to their true spiritual identity and to their Supreme Creator. He sees their suffering in the material world of repeated birth and death and wants them to be relieved, but it is their own free will as to whether they choose to remain attracted to the material energy or the spiritual. Nonetheless, He provides the necessary instruction such as *Bhagavad-gita* and asks everyone to take shelter of Him. But many are those who pay no attention, nor do they realize the ultimate bliss that is awaiting for them if only they would take up the chanting of the holy name and become receptive to all of the potencies that await them by doing so.

It is the eternal function of the individual soul, the *jivatma*, to be attracted to the all-attractive, infinite Supreme Soul, either directly or to His material energy. It is also the eternal function of the Supreme Being to provide various ways for the materially conditioned souls to become attracted to Him and the multifaceted spiritual energy where they can get a taste of everlasting, infinite, supreme bliss and ecstasy. The easiest and most open doorway to this realm is through the invitation to take to the chanting of the holy name of the Supreme Lord. And this name is distributed throughout the material creation only by the mercy of the Lord's devotees who give this opportunity to as many people as possible. For those who do so and take it seriously, they can rise above the temporary passing pleasures derived from the limited material energy and can come in contact with the eternal, infinite and ultimate bliss that compares to an ocean of nectar. This is the significance of the holy name in the form of the Hare Krishna *maha-mantra*.

THE SIGNIFICANCE OF THE HARE KRISHNA MAHA-MANTRA FOR THIS PRESENT AGE OF KALI-YUGA

There are many Vedic references that specifically recommend the chanting of the Hare Krishna *maha-mantra* as the most effective and advantageous means of reaching spiritual realization and counteracting all the problems of this age of Kali-yuga. Some of these verses are the following:
The *Kali-santarana Upanishad* says:

*hare krsna hare krsna krsna krsna hare hare
hare rama hare rama rama rama hare hare
iti shodashakam namnam kali-kalmasha-nashanam
natah parataropayaha sarva-vedeshu drshyate*

"After searching through all of the Vedic literature one cannot find a method of religion more sublime for this age than the chanting of Hare Krishna."

The *Kali-santarana Upanishad* goes on to say, "These sixteen words--Hare Krishna, Hare Krishna, Krishna Krishna, Hare Hare / Hare Rama, Hare Rama, Rama Rama, Hare Hare--are especially meant for counteracting the ill effects of the present age of quarrel and anxiety."

"All mantras and all processes for self-realization are compressed into the Hare Krishna *maha-mantra*." (*Narada-pancharatra*)

"The self-realization which was achieved in the Satya millennium by meditation, in the Treta millennium by the performance of different sacrifices, and in the Dvapara millennium by opulent worship of Lord Krishna [as the Deity in the temple], can be achieved in the age of Kali simply by chanting the holy names, Hare Krishna." (*Bhag.*12.3.52)

"In the other three yugas--Satya, Treta and Dvapara--people perform different types of spiritual activities. Whatever results they achieve in that way, they can achieve in Kali-yuga simply by chanting the Hare Krishna *maha-mantra*." (*Cc.*Madhya, 20.343)

"In this age there is no use in meditation, sacrifice and temple worship. Simply by chanting the holy name of Krishna--Hare Krishna, Hare Krishna, Krishna Krishna, Hare Hare / Hare Rama, Hare Rama, Rama Rama, Hare Hare--one can achieve perfect self-realization." (*Vishnu Purana* 6.2.17)

"Living beings who are entangled in the complicated meshes of birth and death can be freed immediately by even unconsciously chanting the holy name of Krishna, which is feared by fear personified." (*Bhag.*1.1.14)

"Those who are actually advanced in knowledge are able to appreciate the essential value of this age of Kali. Such enlightened persons worship Kali-yuga because in this fallen age, all perfection of life can easily be achieved by the performance of *sankirtana* [the congregational chanting of Krishna's holy names]." (*Bhag.*11.5.36)

The *Narayana-samhita* verse, as confirmed by Madhvacharya in his commentary on the *Mundaka Upanishad*, also states:

dvapariyair janair vishnuh pancharatrais tu kevalaiha
kalua tu nama-matrena pujyate bhagavan harihi

Which means, "In the [previous age of] Dvapara-yuga people should worship Lord Vishnu only by the regulative principles of the *Narada-pancharatra* and other such authorized books. In the [present] age of Kali, however, people should simply chant the holy names of the Supreme Personality of Godhead, Bhagavan."

This is similar to the verse in the *Brihan-naradiya Purana* (38.97), which says:

dhyayan krite yajan yajnais
tretayam dvapare 'rcayan
yad apnoti tad apnoti
kalua sankirtya keshavam

"Whatever is achieved in Satya-yuga by meditation, in Treta-yuga by offering ritual sacrifices, and in Dvapara-yuga by temple worship, is achieved in Kali-yuga by chanting the names of Lord Keshava [Krishna] congregationally."

This point is so important that it is also mentioned in the *Vishnu Purana* (6.2.17), the *Padma Purana* (Uttara-khanda 72.25), and in the *Srimad-Bhagavatam* (12.3.51), which says, "My dear King, although Kali-yuga is an ocean of faults, there is still one good quality about this age; Simply by chanting the Hare Krishna *maha-mantra*, one can become free from material bondage and be promoted to the transcendental kingdom."

Another verse in the *Bhagavatam* (8.23.16) explains this further, "There may be discrepancies in chanting the mantras and observing regulative principles, and, moreover, there may be discrepancies in regard to time, place, person, and paraphernalia. But when Your Lordship's holy name is chanted, everything becomes faultless."

So from the above evidence taken from various Vedic sources, we can understand that each *yuga* or age has its recommended process for spiritual success. In Satya-yuga it was the long process of meditation when people lived for many years and could practice such a method. In Treta-yuga it was by elaborate rituals. In Dvapara-yuga the recommended process was by extensive worship to the Deities in the temples. But in Kali-yuga, humanity hardly has the wealth, stamina, long life, mental equilibrium, or general facility to do any of that. Therefore, it is recommended that you simply and easily chant the holy names of the Hare Krishna mantra because no other religious process is as powerful or illuminating, or as joyfully performed for the fallen souls.

This is why the *Brihan-naradiya Purana* (38.126) also explains:

> *harer nama harer nama*
> *harer namaiva kevalam*
> *kalau nasty eve nastya eve*
> *nastya eva gatir anyatha*

"Chant the holy names, chant the holy names, chant the holy names of the Lord, for in this age of quarrel and confusion, there is no other way, there is no other way, there is no other way."

So, it is found in the Vedic literature that chanting the holy names of God is recommended as the most effective and easiest process for becoming spiritually realized in this age of Kali-yuga. This is why it is called the *yuga-dharma*, which means the main spiritual process for this age of Kali. And as we can plainly see by a simple survey, almost every religion and spiritual path in this age recommends the chanting or singing of the Lord's names and glories, no matter whether it is Christianity, Judaism, Islam, Hinduism, or so many others. All accept the idea of glorifying God by calling and singing His names.

Out of so many processes of spiritual development that can be found within the Vedic tradition, and which still can be done if a person wants to do them, it is said that, "In this age of Kali there is no other religious principle than the chanting of the holy name, which is the essence of all Vedic hymns. This is the purport of all scriptures." (*Cc*.Adi. 7.74)

So no matter what else you may include in your spiritual development, you should also include the chanting of the holy names of Krishna to reach spiritual success.

The *Narada-pancharatra* also describes in the *trayo vedah shad-angani* verse: "The essence of all Vedic knowledge--comprehending the three kinds of Vedic activity [*karma-kanda, jnana-kanda* and *upasana-kanda*, which means the material, intellectual and mental kinds of activities], the *chandah* or Vedic hymns, and the processes for satisfying the demigods--is included in the eight syllables Hare Krishna, Hare Krishna. This is the reality of all Vedanta. The chanting of the holy name is the only means to cross the ocean of nescience."

The *Srimad-Bhagavatam* (11.5.32), in its reference to worshiping Sri Chaitanya Mahaprabhu who was recognized as the most recent *avatara* of the Lord, and who started the movement to propagate the chanting of the holy name of Krishna just 500 years ago, is very clear when it says, "In the age of Kali, intelligent persons perform congregational chanting to worship the incarnation of Godhead who constantly sings the name of Krishna. Although His complexion is not blackish, He is Krishna Himself. He is accompanied by His associates, servants, weapons, and confidential companions."

This chanting is the sublime and easy way to attain spiritual realization, so easy in fact that it is one of the advantages of being born in this difficult age of Kali-yuga.

Chapter Four

Even beings from the higher planetary systems wish to take birth on earth in this yuga simply to utilize the favorable conditions for engaging in this process. As the *Srimad-Bhagavatam* (11.5.36-40) describes, "Those who are actually advanced in knowledge are able to appreciate the essential value of this age of Kali. Such enlightened persons worship Kali-yuga because in this fallen age, all perfection of life can easily be achieved by the performance of *sankirtana* [the congregational chanting of the Lord's holy names.]

"Indeed, there is no higher possible gain for embodied souls forced to wander throughout the material world than the Supreme Lord's *sankirtana* movement, by which one can attain the supreme peace and free oneself from the cycle of repeated birth and death.

"My dear King, the inhabitants of Satya-yuga and other ages eagerly desire to take birth in this age of Kali, since in this age there will be many devotees of the Supreme Lord, Narayana. These devotees will appear in various places, but will be especially numerous in South India. O master of men, in the age of Kali those persons who drink the waters of the holy rivers of Dravida-desha, such as the Tamraparni, Kritamala, Payasvini, the extremely pious Kaveri, and the Pratichi Mahanadi, will almost all be pure-hearted devotees of the Supreme Personality of Godhead, Vasudeva [Krishna]."

In this way, Kali-yuga, wherein quarrel and confusion abound, can become like the golden age of Satya-yuga by bringing the spiritual vibration into our midst through the chanting of the holy names of Krishna. Such is the power of the Hare Krishna *maha-mantra*. As the *Vishnu-dharma* describes:

> *kalau krita-yugam tasya*
> *kalis tasya krite yuge*
> *yasya chetasi govindo*
> *hridaye yasya nachyutaha*

"For one who has Lord Govinda in his heart, Satya-yuga becomes manifest in the midst of Kali-yuga, whereas conversely even Satya-yuga becomes Kali-yuga for one who does not have the infallible Lord in his heart."

CHAPTER FIVE

The Maha-Mantra is the Best Means for Spiritual Realization

When instructing King Pariksit, as described in *Srimad-Bhagavatam* (2.1.11-13), the great sage Shukadeva Gosvami said, "O King, constant chanting of the holy name of the Lord after the ways of the great authorities is the doubtless and fearless way of success for all, including those who are free from all material desires, those who are desirous of all material enjoyment, and also those who are self-satisfied by dint of transcendental knowledge. What is the value of a prolonged life which is wasted, inexperienced by years in this world? Better a moment of full consciousness, because that gives one a start in searching after his supreme interest."

The reason that chanting the Lord's names is such an effective process is because the Lord and His names are identical: they are the same spiritual energy. So instead of trying to first empty the mind of all thoughts and desires, which is a typical part of the process of meditation, we simply fill the mind with the spiritual vibration of the holy names of the Supreme. By chanting Hare Krishna we are in immediate contact with God. If we chant someone else's name, we cannot enjoy their association because the name and the person are different. For example, by chanting "water, water, water," we do not quench our thirst because water and the name are two different things. But in the spiritual world everything is absolute. Krishna is nondifferent from His names and, therefore, we can feel His presence simply by chanting His names. This is further elaborated in the *Caitanya-caritamrita* (Madhya-lila 17.131-133) that explains that there is no difference between the Lord's name, form, or personality, and they are all transcendentally sweet. Krishna's name is the same as Krishna Himself, and is not material in any way. It gives spiritual benedictions and is full of pleasure. But in the material world everything is different.

Furthermore, the *Caitanya-caritamrita* (Adi-lila 17.22) and the *Padma Purana* also explain that the Hare Krishna *maha-mantra* is the sound incarnation of Krishna, and anyone who chants this mantra is in direct association with Krishna and is delivered from the clutches of the material energy.

It is explained that because chanting the names of God brings us in direct contact with God in proportion to the chanter's purity, this process of self-realization is the way of success for everyone. Furthermore, simply by relying on the chanting of the holy names of God, one need not depend upon other processes, rituals, paraphernalia, or persons. One does not even have to be initiated by a spiritual master to chant the *maha-mantra*. As the *Caitanya-caritamrita* (Madhya-lila 15.108) says, one does not have to take initiation, but only has to chant the holy names. Thus, deliverance is available to even the lowest of people.

Herein is evidence that the Hare Krishna *maha-mantra* is so powerful that one who sincerely takes shelter of it, regardless of their condition, will attain all the desired results of connection with the Supreme. The *Skanda Purana* gives further evidence of how powerful is the *maha-mantra*:

> The name of the Lord need not be chanted with regard to place, time, circumstantial conditions, preliminary self-purification or any other factors. Rather, it is completely

independent of all other processes and rewards all the desires of those who eagerly chant it.

Therefore, without a doubt, the Hare Krishna mantra is the most potent mantra one can utilize for spiritual upliftment. The *Caitanya-caritamrita* also points out that one is freed of all sinful reactions simply by chanting Krishna's names. And all the nine types of devotional service are completed by this process. Thus, in Kali-yuga only the chanting of the holy names is necessary for worshiping the Lord. (*Cc.* Madhya-lila, 15.107) However, if one is not able to chant purely or follow the regulations for chanting, it is recommended that one get further guidance from a bona fide spiritual master.

Therefore, in Kali-yuga, the chanting of the holy names is certainly the most practical and effective process for the conditioned souls. It is also the easiest process whether one finds himself in Kali-yuga, Satya-yuga, Treta-yuga, or Dvapara-yuga. Regardless of what age one may be living in, the process of chanting the holy names is always recommended for everyone. The *Vaisakha-mahatmya* section of the *Padma Purana* explains, "The names of the Supreme Lord who has the disc as His weapon should be glorified always and everywhere."

However, the *Srimad-Bhagavatam* (11.5.36-37 and 12.3.51) describes that since the age of Kali is the most difficult, where men have short durations of life, it is also the most fortunate age. Why? Because those who are wise know the value of this age of Kali because, in spite of the fallen nature of this age, the spiritual perfection of life can be attained by the easy process of *sankirtana*, the congregational chanting of Krishna's holy names. No better position can be found to attain freedom from material existence and entrance into the spiritual kingdom than joining the Lord's *sankirtana* movement.

Even those living in other ages desire to take birth in Kali-yuga to take advantage of this special concession of a speedy delivery from the cycle of birth and death through the process of *sankirtana*. This is confirmed in *Srimad-Bhagavatam* (11.5.38) where we find it said that those who live during Satya-yuga and other ages wish to be born in Kali-yuga just to take advantage of associating with the devotees of Lord Narayana, who are especially found in South India.

"In this way, the most perfect penance to be executed in this world is the chanting of the name of Lord Sri Hari. Especially in the age of Kali, one can satisfy the Supreme Lord Vishnu by performing *sankirtana*." (*Caturmasya-mahatmya* section of the *Skanda Purana*)

The fact of the matter, as further related in the *Bhagavatam* (3.33.6-7), is that regardless of what one's present situation is, if a person once speaks about the activities and chants the holy names of the Supreme, or hears about and remembers Him, he becomes eligible to engage in the Vedic rituals. And how much more glorious are those who regularly chant the holy names. Such people are indeed worshipable, for they must have performed all kinds of austerities, achieved the characteristics of the Aryans, studied the *Vedas*, bathed at all the holy places of pilgrimage, and done whatever else is required.

When the great sage Narada Muni was explaining to Srila Vyasadeva the means by which he became enlightened, he said, "It is personally experienced by me that those who are always full of cares and anxieties due to desiring contact of the senses with their objects [of attraction] can cross the ocean of nescience [illusory darkness] on a most suitable boat--the constant chanting of the transcendental names and activities of the Personality of Godhead. It is true that by practicing restraint of the senses by the yoga system one can get relief from the disturbances of desire and lust, but this is not sufficient to give satisfaction to the soul, for this [satisfaction] is derived from devotional service to the Supreme Personality." (*Srimad-Bhagavatam* 1.6.34-35)

Lord Krishna goes on to explain to Uddhava that in the association of saintly devotees, there is always the discussion about Him, and those who partake in such hearing and chanting about the Lord's glories are certainly purified of all sins. In this way, whoever hears, chants and respectfully opens his heart to these topics about the Lord becomes faithfully dedicated to Him. Thus, he achieves devotional service to Lord Krishna. Then, as Lord Krishna Himself asks, "What more remains to be accomplished for the perfect devotee after achieving devotional service unto Me, the Supreme Absolute Truth, whose qualities are innumerable and who am the embodiment of all ecstatic experience?" (*Bhag.* 11.26.28-30)

As further related by Sukadeva Gosvami, "A person who with faith engages in chanting the glories of these various pastimes and incarnations of Vishnu, the Lord of lords, will gain liberation from all sins. The all-auspicious exploits of the all-attractive incarnations of Lord Shri Krishna, the Supreme Personality of Godhead, and also the pastimes He performed as a child, are described in this *Srimad-Bhagavatam* and in other scriptures. Anyone who clearly chants these descriptions of His pastimes will attain transcendental loving service unto Lord Krishna, who is the goal of all perfected sages." (*Bhag.* 11.31.27-28)

Sri Suta Gosvami relates that in a conversation between Narada Muni and Sanatkumara, Sanatkumara explained the way to attain freedom from this world, even for the most wayward sinners. Even all those mean men who are destitute of all good ways of behavior, who are of a wicked mind, who are outcaste, who deceive the world, who are intent upon religious hypocrisy, pride, drinking liquor, and wickedness, who are sinful and cruel, who are interested in another man's wealth, wife and sons, become pure if they resort to the lotus-like feet of Vishnu. The name of Vishnu, sure to succeed here, protects those sinful men who transgress even Him who causes divinity, who gives salvation to the immobile beings and the mobile beings. A man who has done all kinds of sins is freed if he resorts to Vishnu. If a contemptible, wicked biped would commit sin against Vishnu, and by chance resorts to His name, he is emancipated due to the (power of the) name (of Vishnu). However, a man falls down due to his sin against (Vishnu's) name, which is the friend of all. (*Padma Purana* 4.25.8-13)

The sage Kavi instructed King Nimi that the holy names of the Supreme Lord are all-auspicious because they describe His transcendental birth and pastimes, which He performs for the upliftment and salvation of all conditioned souls. For this reason the Lord's holy names are sung throughout the world. (*Bhag.* 11.2.39)

The *Srimad-Bhagavatam* (6.2.11-12) further explains how chanting the holy names of Krishna is more effective than many of the other processes of spiritual purification, which is a benefit for this age: "By following the Vedic ritualistic ceremonies or undergoing atonement, sinful men do not become as purified as by chanting once the holy name of Lord Hari. Although ritualistic atonement may free one from sinful reactions, it does not awaken [the spiritual attitude of] devotional service, unlike the chanting of the Lord's names, which reminds one of the Lord's fame, qualities, attributes, pastimes, and paraphernalia.

"The ritualistic ceremonies of atonement recommended in the religious scriptures are insufficient to cleanse the heart absolutely because after atonement one's mind again runs toward material activities. Consequently, for one who wants liberation from the fruitive reactions of material activities, the chanting of the Hare Krishna mantra, or glorification of the name, fame and pastimes of the Lord, it is recommended as the most perfect process of atonement because such chanting eradicates the dirt from one's heart completely."

This is the difference in associating with the names of God and other Vedic processes of spiritual purification. The names enter the heart and eradicates the material desire seeds. Other processes may decrease one's karma, or give some enlightenment, but the material or sensual desires in the heart are not fully extinguished. Thus, a person may engage in so many spiritual pursuits and still turn around and continue their own materialistic activities which reduce one's spiritual merit or higher consciousness.

The point is that everyone is looking for happiness of some kind. That is the natural condition of the soul. But it is a matter of attaining a higher state of spiritual happiness from the chanting of the names of God that can alleviate the taste for the sporadic states of sensual or mental happiness that come and go, or are always interrupted by different kinds of distress or misery.

Therefore, in Kali-yuga, one of the highest forms of welfare work that can be done for humanity is to help broadcast the glories of the Lord and to help spread the chanting of His holy names. As described, "My dear Lord, those pious and saintly persons who in this age of Kali hear about Your transcendental activities and also glorify them will easily cross over the darkness of the age of Kali-yuga." (*Bhag.* 11.6.24)

In this way, we can begin to understand how elevated the writer of the Vedic scripture considers those who have adopted the process of chanting Krishna's holy names. However, for those who do not like the chanting of the holy names and blaspheme the process and criticize or try to restrain those who do chant, we can understand that their sentiment is due to their sinful and offensive activities. Such people are said to have no intelligence and work for no useful purpose and simply contribute to the chaos and confusion within society. The *Bhagavatam* (3.9.7) confirms that those who do not engage in the blessed chanting and hearing about the activities of the Supreme are bereft of intelligence and good fortune. They perform sinful activities to enjoy sensual pleasure that lasts only for a short time.

CHANTING THE MAHA-MANTRA PURIFIES THE CONSCIOUSNESS

As mentioned, it is this chanting of the names of Krishna which purifies the consciousness to open the individual to experience the spiritual frequency or transcendental dimension. Of course, there is the immediate joy and pleasure in congregational chanting to sing and dance to the musical sound and melodies of the holy names being chanted. But as one goes deeper, the spiritual vibration begins to clear away the darkness of past karma, bad habits, habitual thought patterns, or old attachments, and brings one to experience the real happiness on the spiritual platform. This is another reason why it is said to be the easiest spiritual process for this age.

In this way, the chanting cleanses the dust from the heart, after which the person can realize the importance of the holy name. Of course, if a person is not interested in changing his habits or consciousness, then it is not possible for a person to fully experience the positive and spiritual effects of the name of Krishna. But if a person takes it sincerely, the association of the holy name of Krishna will purify one from the effects of his bad karma.

How the holy name effects us is that it is eternally situated in pure goodness. It is the transcendental name of the Lord and is non-different from the Lord. It actually descends from the spiritual world. So it has the same transcendental frequency when it is chanted properly. Associating with the name through chanting removes the unwanted things from the heart, which softens the heart and evokes compassion for all souls and the desire to remove the cause of suffering for all living beings. It also makes the propensity to engage in impious activities subside. (*Sri Harinama Cintamani*, p.67)

In this way, the chanting purifies the heart and consciousness of anyone who takes it seriously, and brings one's spiritual awareness to a progressively higher level. As the chanting becomes more serious, the effects become deeper. Then the bhakti-yogi can perceive the personality of the holy name and continues to perceive increasingly higher levels of the spiritual dimension all around him.

Srivas Thakur, as noted in the *Caitanya-caritamrita* (Adi.17.96), said, "Anyone who takes to Your holy name vanquishes ten million of his offenses immediately."

The very last verse in the *Srimad-Bhagavatam* (12.13.23) also explains, "I offer my respectful obeisances unto the Supreme Lord, Hari, the congregational chanting of whose holy names destroys all sinful reactions, and the offering of obeisances unto whom relieves all material suffering."

Therefore, the chanting of the holy names burns away the sinful reactions of the foolish things we have done in our lives, as further described: "As fire burns dry grass to ashes, so the holy name of the Lord, whether chanted knowingly or unknowingly, burns to ashes, without fail, all the reactions of one's sinful activities. If a person unaware of the effective potency of a certain medicine takes that medicine or is forced to take it, it will act even without his knowledge because its potency does not depend on the patient's understanding. Similarly, even though one does not know the value of chanting the holy name of the Lord, if one chants knowingly or unknowingly, the chanting will be very effective." (*Bhag*.6.2.18-19)

In the *Brihad-vishnu Purana* it says:

namno hi yavati shaktihi
papa-nirharane hareh
tavat kartum na shaknoti

patakam pataki naraha

"Simply by chanting one name of Hari, a sinful man can counteract the reactions to more sins than he is able to commit."

In the *Garuda Purana* it is also described:

*avashenapi yan-namni
kirtite sarva-patakaihai
puman vimuchyate sadyaha
simha-trastair mrigair iva*

"If one chants the holy name of the Lord, even in a helpless condition or without desiring to do so, all the reactions of his sinful life depart, just as when a lion roars, all the small animals flee in fear."

There is also the story of Ajamila in the sixth Canto of the *Bhagavatam*. Ajamila was known as an extremely sinful person, but fortunately he named his son Narayana. And because he would chant the name so often when calling his son, it was as if he was practicing the chanting of it so that even at the time of death he would call it out. So when he was leaving his body, he became very afraid and in earnest he called for his son, Narayana. By doing so, as the Vishnudutas [soldiers of Lord Vishnu] explained, "Ajamila has already atoned for all of his sinful actions. Indeed, he has atoned not only for sins performed in one life, but for those performed in millions of lives, for in a helpless condition he chanted the holy name of Narayana. Even though he did not chant purely, he chanted without offense, and therefore he is now pure and eligible for liberation." (*Bhag*.6.3.7)

"Even previously, while eating and at other times, this Ajamila would call his son, saying 'My dear Narayana, please come here.' Although calling the name of his son, he nevertheless uttered the four syllables na-ra-ya-na. Simply by chanting the name of Narayana in this way, he sufficiently atoned for the sinful reactions of millions of lives." (*Bhag*.6.2.8)

"While suffering at the time of death, Ajamila chanted the holy name of the Lord, and although the chanting was directed toward calling his son, he nevertheless returned home, back to Godhead. Therefore, if one faithfully and inoffensively chants the holy name of the Lord, where is the doubt that he will return to Godhead [the spiritual world]?" (*Bhag*.6.2.49)

This is how effective the chanting the Lord's names can be if we chant sincerely. It is even described, "One who has killed a brahmana, one who has killed a cow or who has killed his father, mother or spiritual master can be immediately freed from all sinful reactions simply by chanting the holy name of Lord Narayana. Other sinful persons, such as dog-eaters and *chandalas*, who are less than shudras, can also be freed in this way." (*Bhag*.6.13.8)

Of course, this does not mean we can purposefully engage in such activities and think we can merely chant the holy names and be free from all karmic results. That is called engaging in sinful activities on the strength of chanting the holy names, which is greatly offensive to the holy names. That means the effect of such sinful activities will not go away at all. It is like the elephant who may bathe in the water but then again throws sand over itself when it comes out of the water. However, if we genuinely realize the wrong we have done and begin to chant the holy names in sincere remorse for our previous activities, with the intention to not do such things again, the name will certainly have its positive effects. "Thus worship the Lord, whose name is like the sun, for just as a slight appearance of the sun dissipates the darkness of night, so a slight appearance of the holy name of Krishna can drive away all the darkness of ignorance that arises in the heart due to greatly sinful activities performed in previous lives." (*Bhakti-rasamrita-sindhu* 2.1.103)

"Even a faint light of the holy name of the Lord can eradicate all the reactions of sinful life." (*Cc*.Antya.3.63) It is this way in which it raises our consciousness and extinguishes our bad habits and attachments to materialism.

SELF-REALIZATION THROUGH CHANTING

Another point is that by chanting the names of the Lord, one brings the mind under control and allows one to think and meditate on the Absolute Truth. This is much easier than the process of Raja and Astanga-yoga in which we are meant to empty the mind of all thoughts and sensual stimulation, which eventually allows us to have a glimpse of our real identity. Only after understanding and perceiving our real identity as a spiritual being can we proceed to the next step, which is to perceive the Supersoul within us, which is the localized expansion of the Supreme Being, and then to realize what our connection or relationship is with the Supersoul. The chanting of the names of God brings our consciousness into the connection with God much more quickly, and is a much more attractive process. In fact, it is the names of God that is the vibration of God.

So, instead of trying to empty our mind, we fill it with transcendental and spiritual vibration, which uplifts our consciousness to this spiritual frequency. This not only purifies the mind, our consciousness, but opens the channels of perception so that we can also begin to perceive that same spiritual dimension. Meditation is meant to draw to us that which we meditate on, and such meditation of chanting the holy names brings that spiritual frequency to us very quickly. By chanting the Hare Krishna mantra, one immediately concentrates on the sound incarnation of the Lord and thinks of the Absolute Truth by this process. Thus, he or she can be very quickly elevated to the position of *samadhi* or trance in this way. The Hare Krishna mantra can be chanted by anyone,

Chapter Five

without the consideration of where to sit, or how to meditate. There are no such injunctions as you find in Raja or Astanga-yoga. You simply sit, with body straight, and chant and hear the Hare Krishna mantra. Or you can even stand or walk, and simply chant and listen to the mantra. You can't get much easier than that.

Even while singing and dancing to the melody of the Hare Krishna mantra in a congregational setting, if we are open to receiving the vibration, we can begin to experience its potency very quickly, and our hearts can be filled with joy by the contact with such spiritual vibration and sound.

How the holy names bring one to the spiritual level of perception is described by Srila Bhaktisiddhanta Sarasvati Thakur in his *Anubhasya* commentary to the *Caitanya-caritamrita* (Adi.7.73): "The Name and the Named [meaning Krishna] is not different from one another. Therefore, just as Lord Krishna is the absolute reality, liberated, the embodiment of pure consciousness, a transcendental philosopher's stone, so to is His name. Only through the worship of the Holy Name (*nama-bhajana*) can both one's gross and subtle misidentifications be destroyed. The Vaikuntha name [meaning completely spiritual since the name comes from the spiritual world] alone can save the living being from absorption in thoughts of material sense gratification. Because it is powerful enough to do this, it is called the *mantra-sara*, the essence of all mantras. Every material thing has its name, form, attributes, characteristics, and functions, all of which are subject to arguments and experimental knowledge. The same is not true for the Vaikuntha name; the name, form, attributes, and associates of the Lord are all situated in nonduality." (*Art of Sadhana*, p.147)

This means that the Lord, His characteristics, form, and name are all the same in spiritual substance. For this reason, chanting the holy names of the Lord, or discussing Krishna's characteristics, are the best means of understanding the Absolute Truth and becoming progressively spiritually realized. And one of the best ways to glorify and remember the Lord is to chant and sing His names. As it is explained, "O descendant of King Bharata, one who desires to be free from all miseries must hear about, glorify, and also remember the Personality of Godhead, who is the Supersoul, the controller and savior from all miseries." (*Bhag*.2.1.5)

"O King, it is therefore essential that every human being hear about, glorify and remember the Supreme Lord, the Personality of Godhead, always and everywhere." (*Bhag*.2.2.36)

"Devotional service, beginning with the chanting of the holy name of the Lord, is the ultimate religious principle for the living entity in human society." (*Bhag*.6.3.22)

"Simply by chanting the holy name of Krishna, one is relieved from all the reactions of a sinful life. One can complete the nine processes of devotional service by chanting the holy name." (*Cc*.Mad.15.107)

The nine processes of bhakti-yoga or devotional service include hearing, chanting, remembering the Lord, serving, worshiping the Lord, praying, obeying, maintaining friendship with the Lord, and surrendering everything to the Lord. But simply chanting the holy names, which automatically includes hearing, is the way that completes every other of the nine processes. So the way to reach the heights of spiritual realization, along with everything else you may include, is through the chanting of the holy names. But this means that one must chant offenselessly, which we will discuss more later. As this continues, it awakens the dormant love of God in the heart. This is beyond merely realizing one's spiritual position as a soul within the body. This is the ultimate level of purity and spiritual realization, that by purely chanting the holy names we can be free from our karma, which paves the way to awaken our loving relationship with God.

Chapter Five

"Simply chanting the Hare Krishna *maha-mantra* without offenses vanquishes all sinful activities. Thus pure devotional service, which is the cause of love of Godhead, Krishna *prema*, becomes manifest." (*Cc.*Adi.8.26 & *Cc.*Antya 4.70-1)

"By chanting the holy name of the Lord, one [becomes materially free and] dissolves his entanglement in material activities. After this, one becomes very attracted to Krishna, and thus dormant love for Krishna is awakened." (*Cc.*Mad.15.109)

The importance of this is further emphasized in the *Bhagavatam* (11.2.40), "By chanting the holy name of the Supreme Lord, one comes to the stage of love of Godhead. Then the devotee is fixed in his vow as an eternal servant of the Lord, and he gradually becomes very much attached to a particular name and form of the Supreme Personality of Godhead. As his heart melts with ecstatic love, he laughs loudly or cries and shouts. Sometimes he sings and dances like a madman, for he is indifferent to public opinion."

In this way, the bhakti-yogi realizes that he has reached the ultimate position of his or her psychological and spiritual development, the realization of which also gives the devotee great joy. He also realizes that the holy name is the most precious treasure in the Lord's storehouse. It is the chief means that awakens love of God, which is the prerequisite for attaining the spiritual domain. Furthermore, the Supreme Being has four characteristic features that can attract us, namely His name, form, qualities, and activities. But the name is original and superior because it is through the name that we are awarded the cognition of the other three features. Therefore, especially for a Vaishnava or Krishna devotee, chanting the holy name is the prime religious activity. It can accomplish everything else.

Since chanting the holy name of Krishna is so important, we should endeavor with great determination to take shelter of the holy name in all times and circumstances.

The more we do this, the more the holy name, which is an incarnation of Krishna, will bestow His mercy on us and relieve us of all the unwanted things in our hearts and bring all auspiciousness. When we become purified and develop a love for Krishna's name, then feelings of *raga* also become possible, which is the feeling of attachment for a relationship with the Lord.

In one of the songs by Srila Bhaktivinoda Thakur called *"Krishna-nama dhare kata bala?"* in his book *Saranagati*, he says, "When the name is even slightly revealed, it shows me my own spiritual form and characteristics. It steals my mind and takes it to Krishna's side. When the Name is fully revealed, it takes me directly to Vraja, where it shows me my personal role in the eternal pastimes."

This means that as we purify or spiritualize our consciousness, our own devotional or Vraja mood is revealed, along with how we fit into the eternal pastimes of Krishna in His supreme abode. This is and leads to the perfectional stage of spiritual realization. (*Art of Sadhana*, p.26)

IMPORTANT BENEFITS OF CHANTING THE HOLY NAMES

The main benefit of chanting the holy names is that it immediately fixes the mind on the Absolute Truth without the need for clearing the mind of all thoughts as is necessary with other forms of meditation. In that way it is very easy. Plus, anyone can do it. "One does not have to undergo initiation or execute the activities required before initiation. One simply has to vibrate the holy name on the lips. Thus even a man of the lowest class [*chandala*] can be delivered." (*Cc*.Mad.15.108)

To emphasize this point, Srila Rupa Goswami also says in his *Padyavali* (29), "The holy name of Lord Krishna is an attractive feature for many saintly, liberal people. It is the annihilator of all sinful reactions and is so powerful that save for the dumb who cannot chant it, it is readily available to everyone, including the lowest type of man, the *chandala*. The holy name of Krishna is the controller of the opulence of liberation, and it is identical with Krishna. Simply by touching the holy name with one's tongue, immediate effects are produced. Chanting the holy name does not depend on initiation, pious activities or the *purashcharya* regulative principles generally observed before initiation. The holy name does not wait for all these activities. It is self-sufficient."

Many Vedic mantras are not allowed to be given to a person without them being initiated by a guru into its chanting. It is this initiation which awakens one's transcendental knowledge by spiritual purification, or which gives the means to invoke the power of the mantra. But for chanting the Hare Krishna mantra, all that is required is faith.

This is the glory of the chanting process, it is clearly open to anyone. In the previous *yugas*, there were so many prerequisites that had to be accomplished before a person could properly engage in the various forms of spiritual development. But it is like Krishna is saying that since the age of Kali-yuga is so bad, like you are My worst son, so I will give you the easiest process. Nonetheless, being initiated by a pure devotee spiritual master will certainly help one's chanting, and propel him or her forward in spiritual development. His spiritual consciousness and the potency of the mantra will awaken much sooner. Still, whether initiated or not, a person can follow the instructions of such a guru for his or her ultimate benefit, and chant the Hare Krishna mantra.

THE HOLY NAME IS ALWAYS EFFECTIVE

"As a fire burns dry grass to ashes, so the holy name of the Lord, whether chanted knowingly or unknowingly, burns to ashes, without fail, all the reactions to one's sinful activities.

"If a person unaware of the effective potency of a certain medicine takes that medicine or is forced to take it, it will act even without his knowledge because its potency does not depend on the patient's understanding. Similarly, even though one does not know the value of chanting the holy name of the Lord, if one chants knowingly or unknowingly, the chanting will be very effective." (*Bhag*.6.2.18-19)

Even when one chants the holy name in a joking way, it still has its effect. Or even when a person chants it to mean something else, some potency is still there. For example, when we say something about the Ramada Inn, which is a popular hotel chain, the name *Rama* is there. As the *acharya* or authority on the chanting of the holy name Haridasa Thakur said, "The chanting of the Lord's holy name to indicate something other than the Lord is an instance of *namabhasa*. Even when the holy name is chanted in this way, its transcendental power is not destroyed." (*Cc*.Antya.3.55)

Namabhasa is the stage above offensive chanting when a person still gets a dim reflection of the power of the holy name. It is not pure chanting, yet some effect is still there, though it may not produce the full result. Nonetheless, when we begin to chant without offenses, being sincere and alert to our chanting, then the power of the holy name and its effect on us becomes much stronger. But as it is said in the *Caitanya-caritamrita* (Antya 3.60), if a devotee once utters the holy name of the Lord, and it enters the ear, which is the channel of aural reception, and then penetrates the mind, that holy name will certainly deliver him from material bondage, whether vibrated properly or improperly, with correct or incorrect grammar. The potency of the holy name is certainly great.

This is also repeated in the *Srimad-Bhagavatam* (6.16.44), "My Lord, it is not impossible for one to be immediately freed from all material contamination by seeing

You. Not to speak of seeing You personally, merely by hearing the holy name of Your Lordship only once, even *chandalas*, men of the lowest class, are free from all material contamination. Under the circumstances, who will not be freed from material contamination simply by seeing You?"

So here the potency of the holy name becomes clear. Furthermore, it is most purifying spiritually while we chant the holy name during our life, but if we can chant it just before or while we are leaving this body at the time of death, it will certainly transfer us into a higher dimension in our next existence. This is why we must practice chanting the holy names throughout our lives, and especially during times of danger when we may be forced to leave this body, and that way we will be more likely to remember to chant the holy names while we leave this body. It is not always possible to leave this world in a smooth transition, but we may leave through some sudden and unexpected incident. Therefore we must be ready to chant the holy name of Krishna at the time of death so we can be transferred to the next best situation possible. This is also explained in the *Srimad-Bhagavatam* (3.9.15), "Let me take shelter of the lotus feet of Him whose incarnations, qualities and activities are mysterious imitations of worldly affairs [which means they are not of this world at all]. One who invokes His transcendental names, even unconsciously, at the time he quits this life, is certainly washed immediately of the sins of many, many births and attains Him without fail."

It is this way that the holy name propels a person into higher realms of existence if he or she chants the holy names at the time of death, as explained herein, "If one chants the holy name of Hari and then dies because of an accidental misfortune, such as falling from the top of a house, slipping and suffering broken bones while traveling on the road, being bitten by a serpent, being afflicted with pain and high fever, or being injured by a weapon, one is immediately absolved from having to enter hellish life, even though he is sinful.

"Authorities who are learned scholars and sages have carefully ascertained that one should atone for the heaviest sins by undergoing a heavy process of atonement, and one should atone for lighter sins by undergoing lighter atonement. Chanting the Hare Krishna mantra, however, vanquishes all the effects of sinful activities, regardless of whether heavy or light." (*Bhag*.6.2.15-16)

In the *Skanda Purana* it also says:

> *sakrid uccharitam yena*
> *harir ity akshara-dvayam*
> *baddha-parikaras tena*
> *mokshaya gamanam prati*

"By one chanting the holy name of the Lord, which consists of the two syllables *ha-ri*, one guarantees his path to liberation."

CHANTING THE HOLY NAMES IS BEST PROCESS EVEN FOR HOUSEHOLDERS

Chanting the holy names is so easy but powerful, it is recommended that even householders, or those who are married and with children, can achieve success by this chanting process. Usually householders are completely preoccupied with materialistic pursuits, such as trying to make money, maintaining a job, taking care of one's health, overseeing the progress and growth of the children, taking care of the house, and so many other things. They hardly have time for anything truly spiritual. Nonetheless, the chanting of the holy names is so powerful that even householders can reach spiritual success if they simply engage in this process. In fact they can reach the same spiritual success as the renounced sages. This is explained by the great sage Narada Muni to Maharaja Yudhishthira when he was outlining the instruction for a civilized human society, "The process of chanting the holy name of the Lord is so powerful that by this chanting even householders [*grihasthas*] can very easily gain the ultimate result achieved by persons in the renounced order. Maharaja Yudhishthira, I have now explained to you that process of religion." (*Bhag*.7.15.74)

An example of this is found in the *Caitanya-caritamrta* (Madhya, 3.188-90) wherein Sri Chaitanya was addressing many of His followers who were married householders, in which He explained that they could easily attain the goal of spiritual realization simply by staying at home and molding their lives to include the chanting of the *maha-mantra*. "Lord Sri Chaitanya Mahaprabhu offered respects to all the devotees present from Navadvipa and other towns, speaking to them as follows.

"'My dear friends, you are all my intimate friends. Now I am begging a favor of you. Please give it to Me.'

"Lord Chaitanya requested them all to return home and begin chanting the holy name congregationally. He also requested them to worship Krishna, chant His holy name and discuss His holy pastimes." Thereafter He requested that He be allowed to go to Jagannatha Puri.

In the purport to this verse, Srila A. C. Bhaktivedanta Swami Prabhupada explains very nicely that for the average persons, by Sri Chaitanya's instructions, they can simply take up the process of chanting the Hare Krishna *maha-mantra* at home: "The society of Sri Chaitanya Mahaprabhu, the Hare Krishna Movement, is very nicely explained by Lord Chaitanya Mahaprabhu authoritatively. It is not that everyone has to take sannyasa like Sri Chaitanya Mahaprabhu. Everyone can execute the means of Krishna consciousness at home, as ordered by the Lord. Everyone can congregationally chant the holy name of Krishna, the Hare Krishna *maha-mantra*. One can also discuss the subject matter of *Bhagavad-gita* and *Srimad-Bhagavatam* and install Deities of Radha-Krishna or Gaura-Nitai or both and worship them very carefully in one's own home. It is not that we have to open different centers all over the world. Whoever cares for the Krishna consciousness movement can install Deities at home and, under superior guidance, worship the Deity regularly, chanting the *maha-mantra* and discussing *Bhagavad-gita* and *Srimad-Bhagavatam*. We are actually teaching in our classes how to go about this. One who feels that he is not yet ready to live in a temple or undergo strict regulative principles in the temple--especially householders who live with wife and children--can start a center at home by installing the Deity, worshiping the Lord morning and evening, chanting Hare Krishna and discussing *Bhagavad-gita* and *Srimad-Bhagavatam*. Anyone can do this at home without difficulty, and Sri Chaitanya Mahaprabhu requested all the devotees present there to do so."

However, to attain all of these benefits means that we have to chant with faith, sincerity and devotion. We have to have some respect for the holy name or our chanting will not produce the fullest effects that we may wish. It is still potent under any circumstance, but due regard while chanting the holy names will produce deeper benefits.

When we understand that the Lord and His name are identical, we can see the personality of the name the more we give it proper respect. It also has divine qualities like forgiveness, serenity, compassion, kindness, love, wisdom, etc., and all of these qualities will also rub off on us as we associate with the name through chanting or singing it.

LORD VISHNU'S NAMES ARE MORE POWERFUL THAN THE GREATEST HOLY PLACES

The power of the Lord's holy names is exhibited in the following story. It is described in the *Padma Purana* that many years ago when asked by the sages at the forest of Naimisharanaya which one single act will bring the fruit of

Chapter Five

visiting the many holy places, Suta Gosvami answered in this way: Out of so many rituals and rites that are prescribed, only one is superior. There is no doubt that one who has devotion to Lord Vishnu has undoubtedly conquered everything. Hari, [Vishnu, Krishna], the Lord of all gods, should alone be propitiated. The goblin of sin will perish by means of the great sacred hymns in the form of the names of Vishnu. There is no doubt that those with pure hearts, going around Vishnu even once, get (the fruit of) having bathed at all the holy places. A man would obtain the fruit of (having visited) all holy places by seeing Vishnu's image. Chanting the excellent name of Vishnu, a man would obtain (the result) of having chanted all the sacred hymns. A man having once smelt the tulasi plant, the grace of Vishnu, does not see the huge and terrible face of Yama [Yamaraja, the lord of death]. A man having (but) once saluted Krishna does not drink the mother's milk [does not need to be reborn again]. I always repeatedly salute them whose mind is (fixed) on the feet of Vishnu. Even [those of lower tribes, such as] pulkasas, chandalas, or other mleccha tribes, who serve the feet of Vishnu alone are fit to be saluted. Then what about the meritorious and devoted brahmanas and royal sages? Having placed one's devotion in Vishnu, a person does not experience confinement in the womb (is not reborn). A man who with high sounds chants the name of Vishnu purifies the world as does the Ganga [Ganges River]. There is no doubt that a man is freed from sins like murder of a brahmana by seeing (the image of), touching (the feet of), reciting (the name of), and devoting oneself (to Vishnu). Circumambulating (the image of) Hari [Vishnu, Krishna], and loudly chanting His names in a sweet and melodious voice, accompanied with clapping of the hands, a man has struck the sin of murdering a brahmana from his hands. A man becomes pure by just seeing Him, who having narrated His story, would listen to a narrative about Him. Then, O best of sages, how can there be the slightest doubt about such a person's sins. (*Padma Purana* 3.50.1-17)

"O great sages, Vishnu's name is the best holy place of all holy places. Those who have uttered the name of Krishna make the world a holy place. Therefore, O best of sages, they consider nothing more meritorious than this. A man using and holding on his head the remains of offered flowers to Vishnu, would beckon Vishnu, who is the destroyer of grief due to fear of Yamaraja. Undoubtedly, Vishnu (alone) is to be worshiped and saluted. Therefore, see and worship Vishnu only, who has no beginning or end, who is the soul (of everything), and who is unmanifest... Vishnu, the Lord Himself, liberates a fool or a chandala to whom Vishnu is dear. There is none greater than Vishnu, who is like a wild fire for (burning) heaps of sins. A man, even after having committed a terrible sin, is freed by the name of Vishnu. Lord Vishnu, the Father of the worlds, has put greater strength than Himself into His name. Therefore a man looking highly upon Vishnu's name should be devoted to Hari. The name of Vishnu is a great destructive weapon like the thunderbolt in rending the mountain of sins. His feet are fruitful and move for that (only). The hands that worship Him are alone said to be blessed. That head which bends before Hari (Vishnu) is the best part of the body. That is (really) the tongue that extols Vishnu. That is the mind which follows His feet. That is the hair that bristles [stands up in ecstasy] at the utterance of His name. Those are the tears that are shed due to devotion to Lord Vishnu. Oh, people are very much duped by their faults if they do not resort to (Him) by merely chanting His names. Those who though having got a tongue do not utter the name of Vishnu, easily fall [back into the cycles of birth and death] even after having secured the stairway to liberation. Therefore, a man should carefully (please) Lord Vishnu by means of worldly and religious rites [devotional service]. Lord Vishnu is pleased with religious rites, not otherwise. The worship of Vishnu is said to be a holier place than a holy place. A man obtains that fruit by serving Vishnu which he obtains by bathing at and drinking (the water from) all the holy places. Only blessed men worship Vishnu by means of worldly and religious rites [devotional service]. Therefore, O sages, worship Krishna (Vishnu), who is the most auspicious." (*Padma Purana* 3.50.17-39)

CHAPTER SIX

The Great Good Fortune of One Who Chants Hare Krishna

The persons who can engage in the chanting of the Lord's holy names are not ordinary. It is considered that they have already been engaged in spiritual development for some time, even lifetimes, and can now engage in what many of the spiritual texts call the epitome of spiritual progress.

For example, when Chaitanya Mahaprabhu was talking with Prakashananda Sarasvati, He explained that His guru told Him, "You are a fool. You are not qualified to study Vedanta philosophy, and therefore You must always chant the holy name of Krishna. This is the essence of all mantras or Vedic hymns. Simply by chanting the holy name of Krishna, one can obtain freedom from material existence. Indeed, simply by chanting the Hare Krishna mantra one will be able to see the lotus feet of the Lord." (*Cc*.Adi.7.72-3)

Of course, it is not that Sri Chaitanya was a fool, but to exhibit an example that anyone these days is hardly qualified to extensively study Vedanta philosophy, even if they are interested. However, regardless of one's qualifications, anyone can engage in the chanting of the holy names. It goes beyond the need for qualifications. But, if someone does engage in such chanting, it shows how extremely fortunate they are. They had to have engaged in numerous pious activities over the course of their past lives, and now can simply follow the easiest and most effective path for this age. An example of this is found in the *Srimad-Bhagavatam* (3.33.7) where Srimati Devahuti describes to her son, Lord Kapiladeva, "Oh, how glorious are they whose tongues are chanting Your holy name! Even if born in the family of dog-eaters, such persons are worshipable. Persons who chant the holy name of Your Lordship must have executed all kinds of austerities and fire rituals and achieved all the good manners of the Aryans. To be chanting the holy name of Your Lordship, they must have bathed at holy places of pilgrimage, studied the *Vedas*, and fulfilled everything required."

Therefore, it is through this hearing and chanting of the Hare Krishna mantra, and also hearing about and discussing the spiritual qualities of the Supreme Being, that the conditioned souls become most fortunate to have found the path that will bring them to spiritual reality. As Lord Krishna Himself says in the *Srimad-Bhagavatam* (11.20.8), "If somehow or other by good fortune one develops faith in hearing and chanting My glories, such a person, being neither very disgusted with nor attached to material life, should achieve perfection through the path of loving devotion to Me [bhakti-yoga]."

Chaitanya Mahaprabhu asked, "What should all living entities constantly remember?" Ramananda Raya replied, "The chief object of remembrance is always the holy name of the Lord, His qualities and pastimes." (*Cc.* Madhya. 8.252)

"Regardless of time or place, one who chants the holy name, even while eating or sleeping, attains all perfection." (*Cc.* Antya. 20.18)

THE BLISS IN CHANTING THE HOLY NAMES

By now we should begin to see how the holy name of Krishna, when we absorb it into our hearts and consciousness, and when it connects to our soul, can bring us into a higher stage of awareness, happiness and bliss. Of course, if we are absorbed in materialism and our consciousness is focused on bad habits and sensual delights, then we may not be able to taste the joy that can be attained through the holy names. It is like when we are diseased with jaundice. At that time sugar, which is naturally sweet, becomes terribly distasteful. But that is because of our diseased condition. When we are cured of jaundice, then sugar again tastes very sweet. In the same way, in a diseased condition of life, while focused on the materialistic aims and goals, we cannot taste the sweetness of spiritual life, nor the bliss in the chanting of the holy names. But it is the chanting itself that can help relieve us of this diseased condition and give us the cure. Then, what was once bitter becomes like nectar.

This is described in the *Upadeshamrita* (Text 7), "The holy name, character, pastimes, and activities of Krishna are all transcendentally sweet like sugar candy. Although the tongue of one afflicted by the jaundice of *avidya* [ignorance] cannot taste anything sweet, it is wonderful that simply by carefully chanting these sweet names everyday, a natural relish awakens within his tongue, and his disease is gradually destroyed at the root."

As it is further explained, "The Absolute Truth is Sri Krishna, and loving devotion to Sri Krishna exhibited in pure love is achieved through congregational chanting of the holy name, which is the essence of all bliss." (*Cc*.Adi.1.96)

When the happiness of chanting increases, it lifts the person up to a new level of joy, the likes of which he or she has not experienced before. As Sri Chaitanya expressed, "My spiritual master taught Me one verse from *Srimad-Bhagavatam*. It is the essence of all the *Bhagavatam's* instructions; therefore he instructed Me this verse again and again.

"'When a person is actually advanced and takes pleasure in chanting the holy name of the Lord, who is very dear to him, he is agitated and loudly chants the holy name. He also laughs, cries, becomes agitated and chants just like a madman, not caring for outsiders.'

"I firmly believe in those words of My spiritual master, and therefore I always chant the holy name of the Lord, alone and in the association of devotees. That holy name of Lord Krishna sometimes causes Me to chant and dance, and therefore I chant and dance. Please do not think that I intentionally do it. I do it automatically." (*Cc.Adi.* 7.92-96)

Of course, it may take a little while for us to reach this stage of bliss, but it is not only possible, but is also described that this is what happens. In fact, many yogis and people who engage in spiritual activities like yoga, meditation, etc., try to find happiness in the peace of merging into the quiet within them, or in meditation on the Brahman. This can certainly have some positive effects, but it is described that higher than that is the bliss that emanates from the holy name of the Absolute Truth. "Compared to the ocean of transcendental bliss, which is tasted by chanting the Hare Krishna mantra, the pleasure derived from impersonal Brahman realization [*brahmananda*] is like the shallow water in a canal." (*Cc.*Adi.7.97)

So, when we combine those energies of the soul with the Supreme Soul, this brings the greatest ecstasy. This is why it is recommended for the Krishna *bhakta* or devotee to reside in a holy place like Mathura or Mayapur, worship the Deity of the Lord, study and hear the *Srimad-Bhagavatam*, serve and associate with the devotees, and chant the holy names of the Lord, especially as found in the Hare Krishna *maha-mantra*, because by combining the soul with these processes is so potent, that even a little attachment to them can arouse devotional ecstasy even in a beginner. (*Nectar of Devotion*, p.110) Why? Because it connects the soul with the Supreme Being through these devotional activities. All kinds of happiness as found in other sources automatically follow such a pure devotee.

When the devotee is attached to chanting the pure name, he or she will also have the knowledge of the *Vedas* revealed. Gradually, such a person will also attain Krishna *prema*, love of God. The *Vedas* unequivocally declare that by chanting the holy name, one experiences ecstatic bliss, as the holy name is the source of everything, including that supreme spiritual happiness. (*Sri Harinama Cintamani*, p.59)

THE MOST WORSHIPFUL OBJECT IS THE HOLY NAME

When Chaitanya Mahaprabhu was asking Ramanada Raya what is the most worshipable of all objects, Ramanada Raya replied, "The chief worshipable object is the holy name of Radha and Krishna, the Hare Krishna mantra." (*Cc*.Mad.8.256)

So, not only is this *maha-mantra* the vehicle by which we can infuse ourselves with the spiritual vibration of the spiritual world, but out of everything that we hold dear or that is worshipable, the holy name is to be held in the highest esteem. This is why some temples in India are centered around the holy name and have no specific deity. In this way, they chant, sing and discuss the nature of the holy name as their main function. Of course, many are those temples that do have Deities of Radha-Krishna and Krishna's various other forms, and where the chanting and singing of the holy names is one of the essential parts of the worship that goes on there, even having *sankirtana* 24 hours a day. But this shows the importance the holy name has, especially in the form of the Hare Krishna mantra. And as we have mentioned, there are no hard and fast rules to abide by regarding where and how to chant. It can be chanted anywhere, at any time, and in any condition.

Chanting the holy name is direct service to Krishna. And by chanting the names of Krishna in *sankirtana*, a congregational setting, or in solitary meditation in *japa*, a person will develop feelings for Krishna, up to and including Krishna *prema*, ecstatic and intense love. This is the ripened fruit of all revealed scriptures and of chanting the holy names. (*Cc*.Adi.7.83, 86)

This is the ultimate fulfillment of all spiritual pursuits, beyond acquiring knowledge, Brahman realization, or liberation by merging into the Brahman. Attaining this love is what can uplift us to the stage in which we engage in the eternal pastimes of the Lord, either in the Vaikuntha planets or in Goloka Vrindavana. As the *Bhagavata Purana* (1.5.22) points out, "Learned circles have positively concluded that the infallible purpose of the advancement of knowledge, namely [through] austerities, study of the *Vedas*, sacrifice [or rituals], chanting of hymns and charity, culminates in the [hearing of] transcendental descriptions of the Lord, who is defined in choice poetry."

Such pastimes of the Lord can be found in such texts as the *Srimad-Bhagavatam*. Reading or listening to them is the very easy process that is incorporated in bhakti-yoga. This is also why the *Bhagavatam* (2.1.11) points out that for anyone who has developed some spontaneous attachment to the chanting of the holy names of the Lord, or the Hare Krishna mantra, is to be understood as having attained the highest perfectional stage of spiritual success. Also, in the *Adi Purana* Krishna says to Arjuna that anyone who is engaged in chanting My transcendental name must be considered to be always associating with Me. "And I may tell you frankly that for such a devotee I become easily purchased."

The *Padma Purana* also explains that the chanting of Hare Krishna is present only on the lips of a person who has been worshipping Vasudeva [Krishna] for many births. And that there is no difference between the holy name of the Lord and the Lord Himself. As such, the holy name of the Lord is as perfect as the Supreme Being Himself in fullness, purity and eternity. The holy name is no material sound vibration, nor has it any material contamination. (*Nectar of Devotion*, pp.108-9)

The only thing to do then is to reach the stage of chanting offenselessly, wherein the potency of the name can be felt to the highest degree. Materialistic senses cannot properly chant the holy names of the Hare Krishna *maha-mantra*. But by adopting the chanting process, the name itself can purify the devotee so that he may very soon chant offenselessly. So until then, we can certainly have fun by chanting with other devotees and enjoy the saintly association while we help each other raise ourselves to higher and higher spiritual awareness until one day we can float in the ocean of nectar that emanates from Lord Krishna in the form of His names.

This is why Sri Chaitanya has advised that everyone should chant this Hare Krishna mantra just to wipe away the materialistic dust from our hearts that has accumulated over many lifetimes. If this dust is cleansed away, then one can actually understand the importance of the holy name. However, if a person is not inclined to clean away the dust and wants to keep things the way they are in one's materialistic mindset, then it will not be possible to derive the transcendental result from chanting Hare Krishna. Therefore, we should be encouraged to associate with other devotees to maintain our interest and encouragement to develop our spiritual awareness, and our service attitude toward the Lord and His holy names, because this will help us be relieved of the troubles in material existence and experience a higher level of happiness.

This is why the holy names of Krishna are the most worshipable object within this world because hearing Them purifies the inner self. From there we can more easily begin to understand Krishna's form, qualities, characteristics, His associates and then His pastimes. From the chanting of the holy names, all other perfections of spiritual life will come to anyone who takes it seriously. This is the conclusion of spiritual authorities. It is like the shortcut that cuts through all difficulties, both material and spiritual.

Then the most difficult thing to acquire or understand can be attained, which is the loving mood that the residents of the supreme spiritual abode of Goloka Vrindavana have for Lord Krishna. Invoking this mood is the key to being able to enter into the eternal pastimes that go on in the abode of Goloka Vrindavana. And this is all possible by sticking with the chanting of the Lord's names.

CHAPTER SEVEN

Attaining Liberation Through Chanting

It is described that there are certain channels through which the Infinite descends. Similarly, there are certain channels that the living beings can use to escape material existence and attain the spiritual realm. Of course, the final goal of any religious process or yoga system is to get free from material entanglement and enter directly into spiritual existence. This happens easily for one who learns how to purely chant the holy names. This is verified in the *Caitanya-caritamrta* which states that the chanting of the Hare Krishna mantra vanquishes all sins and makes way for the performance of devotional service to begin. The chanting of this *maha-mantra* gives so much spiritual advancement that one easily ends his material existence and attains love of God. (*Cc.* Adi-lila, 8.26, 28) This is the basis of all loving spiritual activities in the transcendental realm.

From everything that has been described so far about the glories of the holy name, such as its potency to purify the mind, to relieve us of material activities and the reactions to sinful acts, as well as to put us in direct contact with the Supreme and reawaken our attraction for Him, it is obvious, especially for this age of Kali-yuga, that the most worshipable object is the Lord's holy names, especially as found in the Hare Krishna *maha-mantra*. The *Bhagavatam* also confirms this by stating that the topmost religious principle for the entire human race is to engage in devotional service beginning with the chanting of the Lord's holy names. Therefore, those who chant the holy names have reached the ultimate position in civilized life and, if they continue on the path, will attain further realizations in spiritual life up to reaching the platform of pure, unadulterated devotional service. (*Bhag,* 6.3.22)

All such transcendental opulences, as stated in the above verses, are attained simply by chanting the Hare Krishna *maha-mantra* without offenses. In this way, one attains the supreme spiritual bliss. The *Caitanya-caritamrita* (Antya-lila, 20.14) explains that by chanting the spiritual names of Krishna one tastes spiritual ecstasy when his love for Krishna awakens. Then one attains Krishna's direct association and feels like he is in an ocean of love.

The name "Krishna" literally means "the greatest pleasure," or "He who is all-attractive." All living entities are looking for pleasure and happiness. God is the storehouse of all pleasure and whatever happiness we feel in this material world is simply due to contact with His energy. However, by chanting His holy names, we can transcend whatever temporary pleasure is found on the material platform and experience actual spiritual happiness by coming in direct contact with the Supreme, the source of all pleasure. The *Caitanya-caritamrita* verifies that simply by chanting the Hare Krishna mantra a person is freed from material life and will be able to see the Lord. (*Cc.* Adi-lila, 7.73)

For one who takes shelter of the *maha-mantra*, he is sure to reach the Supreme because such mystic meditation engages the mind and intelligence in Krishna. By such continued remembrance of Krishna, even though one may seem to be engaged in so many duties, one regains his spiritual consciousness which is the prerequisite for entering back into the spiritual world. As Sri Krishna explains in *Bhagavad-gita* (8.7-8) a person should think of Him as Krishna and carry out one's duty with the mind and intelligence fixed on Him. Thinking and meditating on

Krishna in this undeviated way, one can be sure to reach the divine Supreme Spirit.

From this information we can understand that if we can continue setting some time aside everyday for chanting the *maha-mantra* and spiritualizing our consciousness, we will be prepared for entering the spiritual realm after death. This is the most important aspect of any yoga or religious system--being free from material consciousness and remembering the Supreme at the time we give up our body. This requirement is easily fulfilled simply by remembering the Lord through chanting His holy names. This is confirmed in the *Srimad-Bhagavatam* (3.9.15) which declares that one who takes shelter of Krishna by invoking His spiritual names at the time of leaving the body is cleansed of many lifetimes of sin and attains Krishna without fail.

This is why some people pray that in whatever condition of life they are in, but especially at the time of death, if they can simply remember the holy name of the Lord, they will certainly be uplifted to the spiritual realm. "Dear Lord, we may not be able to remember Your name, form and qualities due to stumbling, hunger, falling down, yawning or being in a miserable diseased condition at the time of death when there is high fever. We therefore pray unto You, O Lord, for You are very affectionate to Your devotees. Please help us remember You and utter Your holy names, attributes and activities, which can dispel all the reactions of our sinful lives." (*Bhag.* 5.3.12)

"... The holy name of the Lord is as powerful as the Lord Himself. Therefore, simply by chanting and hearing the holy name of the Lord, many men can be fully protected from fierce death without difficulty. Thus a devotee is saved." (*Bhag.* 4.10.30)

The most practical example of this is Ajamila, as previously discussed. The *Bhagavatam* (6.2.49) describes that at the time of death Ajamila chanted the Lord's name and returned to the spiritual world, although he was calling for his son, Narayana, and had spent a lifetime in sinful activity.

So where is the doubt that if one seriously chants the Lord's holy name he will return to the spiritual world? This is the power of the spiritual names of the Supreme. Therefore, as the *Bhagavatam* (6.2.46) elaborates, for one who is serious about attaining freedom from material existence, there is nothing more effective than chanting the holy names of the Supreme and discussing His pastimes and qualities. Other processes are not as complete and leave one's mind tainted with passion and ignorance.

Furthermore, all of one's sinful karmic reactions are wiped out simply by chanting the Lord's names and glorifying His qualities and activities. Even if one cannot properly pronounce the holy name, a person will achieve liberation if he chants without offense. (*Bhag.* 6.3.24)

In the chapter of the *Bhagavatam* on the glories of Lord Anantadeva, it is said, "Even if he be distressed or degraded, any person who chants the holy name of the Lord, having heard it from a bona fide spiritual master, is immediately purified. Even if he chants the Lord's name jokingly or by chance, he and anyone who hears him are freed from all sins. Therefore how can anyone seeking disentanglement from the material clutches avoid chanting the holy name of Lord Sesha [an expansion of Lord Krishna]? Of whom else should one take shelter?" (*Bhag.* 5.25.11)

"In great jubilation, Sri Chaitanya Mahaprabhu said, 'My dear Svarupa Damodara and Ramananda Raya, know from Me that chanting of the holy names is the most feasible means of salvation in this age of Kali." (*Cc.* Antya, 20.8)

HOW THE MAHA-MANTRA CAN DELIVER ALL LIVING BEINGS

As a person associates with the Supreme Being through the sound of His holy names or hearing about His qualities, the Lord will begin to enter the heart and change the person's disposition and uplift his or her spiritual awareness. This is confirmed in the *Srimad-Bhagavatam* (12.12.48) where it says, "When people properly glorify the Supreme Personality of Godhead or simply hear about His power, the Lord personally enters their hearts and cleanses away every trace of misfortune, just as the sun removes the darkness or as a powerful wind drives away the clouds."

So here we can understand that the holy names are so potent for those who can sincerely chant them, but what about other living beings like the animals? What can be done for them?

Actually, this was answered in a discussion between Sri Chaitanya Mahaprabhu and Haridasa Thakura. Sri Chaitanya asked, "On this earth there are many living entities, some moving and some not moving. What will happen to the trees, plants, insects and other living entities? How will they be delivered from material bondage?"

Haridasa Thakura replied, "My dear Lord, the deliverance of all moving and nonmoving living entities takes place only by Your mercy. You have already granted this mercy and delivered them. You have loudly chanted the Hare Krishna mantra, and everyone, moving or not moving, has benefitted by hearing it. My Lord, the moving entities who have heard Your loud *sankirtana* have already been delivered from bondage to the material world, and after the nonmoving living entities like trees hear it, there is an echo. Actually, however, it is not an echo; it is the *kirtan* of the nonmoving living entities. All this, although inconceivable, is possible by Your mercy. When loud chanting of the Hare Krishna mantra is performed all over the world by those who follow in Your footsteps, all living entities, moving and nonmoving, dance in ecstatic devotional love." (*Cc.*Antya.3.67-72)

In this way, the Lord acts and provides facility so all living entities can advance spiritually, regardless of who or what they are, as further confirmed in the *Srimad-*

Bhagavatam (10.29.16), "Krishna, the unborn Supreme Personality of Godhead, master of all of the masters of mystic power, delivers all living entities, moving and nonmoving. Nothing is astonishing in the activities of the Lord."

So, by such use of the Hare Krishna mantra, any living being that comes in contact with it gets spiritual benefit. But especially those who understand the significance of the mantra and use it faithfully and sincerely. This is why the spiritual aspirants, those who are advanced in spiritual pursuits, chant the holy names and discuss the pastimes and characteristics of the Supreme Being so devotedly. "Paramahamsas, devotees who have accepted the essence of life, are attached to Krishna in the core of their hearts, and He is the aim of their lives. It is their nature to talk only of Krishna at every moment, as if such topics were newer and newer. They are as attached to such topics as materialists are attached to topics of women and sex." (*Bhag.*10.13.2)

CHAPTER EIGHT

How to Chant the Hare Krishna Maha-Mantra

In learning the best way to chant, the first thing to remember is that all it takes is faith to chant the holy names. It is said that one who has sufficient faith is eligible to chant them. But even without faith, anyone can try it and recognize the joy within the chanting. But with a little experience, a person will want to continue the process. And with this faith, a person will want to become more steady at it and dive more deeply into it.

The *Vishnu-dharma* states that there are no hard or strict rules when it comes to chanting the holy names of the Lord. You can do it at any time or any place, as stated:

>   *na desha-niyamas tatra*
>   *na kala-niyamas tatha*
>   *nocchishtadau nishehash cha*
>   *shri-harer namni lubdhakaha*

"There is no restriction of place or time, nor any injunction forbidding the accepting of remnants of food, etc., when one has become greedy to chant the name of Sri Hari."

Furthermore, anyone can certainly join a group for *sankirtana* chanting of the Hare Krishna mantra, or even pick up a set of beads to chant *japa* quietly for oneself. In any way you chant, it is beneficial and joyful. But there are a few things that will help you get the most out of your chanting,

Chapter Eight

and to bring out the deepest effects of the holy names. So the second point is the mood in which you chant.

"To chant the holy name always, one should be humbler than the grass in the street and devoid of all desire for personal honor, but one should offer all respects to others." (*Cc*.Adi.17.26 & Antya.20.21 & *Sikshasthaka* text 3)

This quality of humility is elaborated as follows: "A devotee engaged in chanting the holy name of the Lord should practice forbearance like that of a tree. Even if rebuked or chastised, he should not say anything to others to retaliate. For even if one cuts a tree, it never protests, nor even if it is drying up and dying does it ask anyone for water." (*Cc*. Adi. 17.27-28)

Sri Chaitanya Mahaprabhu continued, "O Svarupa Damodara Gosvami and Ramananda Raya, hear from Me the symptoms of how one should chant the Hare Krishna *maha-mantra* to awaken very easily one's dormant love for Krishna.

"One who thinks himself lower than the grass, who is more tolerant than a tree, and who does not expect personal honor but is always prepared to give all respect to others, can very easily always chant the holy name of the Lord.

"These are the symptoms of one who chants the Hare Krishna *maha-mantra*. Although he is very exalted, he thinks himself lower than the grass on the ground, and like a tree, he tolerates everything in two ways.

"When a tree is cut down, it does not protest, and even when drying up, it does not ask anyone for water.

"The tree delivers its fruits, flowers and whatever it possesses to anyone and everyone. It tolerates scorching heat and torrents of rain, yet it still gives shelter to others.

"Although a Vaishnava is the most exalted person, he is prideless and gives all respect to everyone, knowing everyone to be the resting place of Krishna.

"If one chants the holy name of Lord Krishna in this manner, he will certainly awaken his dormant love for Krishna's lotus feet." (*Cc*. Antya. 20.20-26)

In this way, the attitude while chanting should be one of humility, that we are like infants crying for our mother, or praying to the Lord for guidance to know what to do in our life. We may have so much material facility, such as wealth, big house, fat bank account, beautiful wife or husband, but if we do not truly know who we are on a spiritual level, we are but fools. We have no reason whatsoever to be proud. It is only by the guidance from the Supreme that we may get the understanding of who we really are and where we are going, or where we should be going. And the only way we can get that is by getting the mercy of the holy name, which will then act on us to open our hearts to the higher wisdom it has to offer. And, in most cases, the only way we get the holy name is through the grace of the pure devotees. Then this will lead us or open us up to the directions that Lord Krishna gives in such texts as the *Bhagavad-gita* and others. And our mood of humility while chanting the holy names will help us attain that.

The best mood in which to chant is the mood of love, asking Krishna for the mercy to get closer to Him. Chanting God's holy names is also a type of admiration or worship, and if this is done with a loving feeling, then that will help open deeper levels of love for God. Of course, such love means without the desire for any personal motive or benefit. It should be done simply to please the Lord. In this way, the yogi should have no desire in his mind while chanting, other than love for the name itself, which is actually love for Krishna. The *japa* should be carried out with love, faith and reverence for the mantra. And the more love there is, the more inwardly focused will be the devotee. If the devotee thinks of anything while chanting, it should be of the form, qualities or pastimes of the Lord. Then the devotee's tongue, ears and mind are all engaged in the chanting process, and his soul will float on the ocean of joy, peace and bliss. When one tastes such feelings, the meditation on the holy names can only go deeper and more inward.

Chapter Eight

For me, when I think of how kind the Lord has been to me in so many arrangements of my life that were made beyond my own capacity, but for getting closer to understand God, or freer from material impediments, or in awakening deeper levels of spiritual awareness, I cannot help but be overcome with emotion while chanting the holy names. It shows that the Lord has taken care of me better than I could take care of myself. It also shows the strong connection there has been throughout my life in my purpose to find God, and that my destiny was also there throughout whatever else I have done in this life. In this way, there is the realization that the Divine is all love, the very embodiment of love. Love is His very nature. He is all mercy, and merely waiting for us to turn toward Him so He can more easily display such compassion and care. Then, in this kind of mood, you can recognize the arrangement and power of God wherever you look. Anywhere in the world is the power of God and God's qualities of compassion, mercy, kindness, care, and concern, all of which we are meant to reflect in our own character the closer we get to God. And anything that does not reflect this is nothing but mankind's absence of God.

The next step is to try to chant without being distracted, especially for chanting *japa* for one's personal meditation. This means two things: first that your chanting is focused on the sound of the holy names, and second, that you start to chant a certain number of names or rounds on your beads every day. If you are distracted, you will be thinking of something else and will also likely just try to complete your chanting without much thought or devotion. It is important to concentrate on the quality of your chanting, and that the name should be pronounced distinctly. If you cannot understand the words you are calling for Krishna, it is likely that He may not understand them either, nor anyone else. Krishna should also be able to understand whose name you are chanting. This way you can begin to taste the nectar of the name. And that is important to increase your faith in the chanting.

If we can chant in the ways we have described so far, we can avoid what is called offensive chanting. So we must know what is offensive chanting, because this will nullify or greatly decrease whatever benefits we would otherwise derive from our chanting.

This is described in the *Hari-bhakti-vilasa* (11.527) as quoted from the *Padma Purana*, "Should someone utter the holy name of the Lord even once, or should he merely remember it or hear it in passing, it will certainly deliver him from material bondage, whether it is correctly or incorrectly pronounced, properly joined, or vibrated in parts. O brahmana, if one uses the holy name for the benefit of the material body, for material wealth and followers, or under the influence of greed or atheism--in other words, if one utters the name with offenses--such chanting will not produce the desired result with the same rapidity."

It is further explained that, "If one chants the exalted holy name of the Lord again and again, and yet his love for the Supreme Lord does not develop and tears do not appear in his eyes, it is evident that because of his offenses in chanting, the seed of the holy name of Krishna does not sprout." (*Cc.* Adi., 8.29-30)

"If one is offensive in the chanting of the Hare Krishna *maha-mantra*, despite his endeavor to chant the holy name for many births, he will not get the love of Godhead which is the ultimate goal of this chanting." (*Cc.*Adi.8.16)

Therefore, "When a person receives the seed of devotional service, he should take care of it by becoming a gardener and sowing the seed in his heart. If he waters the seed gradually by the process of *shravana* and *kirtana* [hearing and chanting the holy names], the seed will begin to sprout." (*Cc.*Madhya, 19.152

"The gardener must defend the creeper by fencing it all around so that the powerful elephant of offenses may not enter.

"Sometimes unwanted creepers, such as the creepers of desires for material enjoyment and liberation from the material world, grow along with the creeper of devotional service. The varieties of such unwanted creepers are unlimited.

"Some unnecessary creepers growing with the bhakti creeper are the creepers of behavior unacceptable for those trying to attain perfection, such as diplomatic behavior, animal killing, mundane profiteering, mundane adoration and mundane importance. All these are unwanted creepers.

"If one does not distinguish between the *bhakti-lata* creeper [the creeper or vine of devotion to Krishna] and the other creepers, the sprinkling of water is misused because the other creepers are nourished while the *bhakti-lata* creeper is curtailed." (*Cc.* Madhya, 19.157-160)

The fact is, offensive chanting is a likely stage of chanting we all go through when we first begin to chant. It is not uncommon. We all chant with the idea that it may improve our health, wealth, peace of mind, interactions with others, and so on, which it will certainly assist in many ways. But that is not the prime purpose of it. However, if the beginner in chanting is not contaminated by atheistic concepts, he still has a good chance of going through this offensive stage and reach a higher level of chanting and feeling reciprocation with the holy name in due time. He is only ignorant of the potency of the name and the real purpose in chanting it. (*Sri Harinama Cintamani*, p. 27) And this can be easily corrected.

There are three stages to chanting: *namaparadha*, which is offensive chanting, then *namabhasa*, or the stage of less offenses or the reflection of the holy name when we are still not chanting properly but getting closer, and then *shuddha-nama*, when we reach the pure chanting of the holy name, which brings liberation.

A few of the offenses in chanting the holy names include chanting without focus or intention, or with a material conception of the holy name, or improper understanding (*sanketa*), chanting in jest or ridicule (*parihasa*), chanting derisively (*stobha*), or with disregard or neglect (*hela*). (*Sri Harinama Cintamani*, p.22)

In fact, if we continue to chant, the holy names themselves will purify us so we can reach the second stage of chanting, or the *namabhasa* stage. "The letters of the holy name have so much spiritual potency that they act even when uttered improperly." (*Cc*.Antya, 3.59)

This *namabhasa* or cleansing stage is not to be underestimated, for it still avails many positive benefits to the individual and increases his piety. It offers him great good fortune, more than religiosity, vows, yoga, rituals, and so on. By chanting, all one's sinful reactions become absolved, and he is freed from the effects of Kali-yuga. Even the miseries brought on by demons, ghosts, evil spirits, and malefic planetary influences can be averted by the power of the holy names. Even if one is destined for the hellish planets, such karma can be counteracted. It is even more powerful than visiting every pilgrimage place, studying all the *Vedas*, or performing all kinds of altruistic work. *Namabhasa* chanting even offers an eternal residence in the spiritual abode of Vaikuntha, especially during the age of Kali-yuga. (*Sri Harinama Cintamani*, p.22) So even this stage offers great opportunity for spiritual advancement.

"In this age of Kali, one cannot attain liberation without taking to the devotional service of the Lord. In this age, even if one does not chant the holy name of Krishna properly, he still attains liberation very easily." (*Cc*.Madhya, 25.30)

This is why, "Sri Chaitanya Mahaprabhu further advised Subuddhi Raya: 'Begin chanting the Hare Krishna mantra, and when your chanting is almost pure, all your sinful reactions will go away. After you chant perfectly, you will get shelter at the lotus feet of Lord Krishna.'" (*Cc*.Madhya, 25.199)

However, there are ten main offenses to the holy name that need to be avoided if we are to advance quickly, and these are:

1. To blaspheme the devotees who have dedicated their lives to the propagation of the holy names of the Lord.
2. To consider the names of the demigods like lord Shiva or lord Brahma to be equal to, or independent of, the name of Lord Vishnu.
3. To disobey the orders of the spiritual master.
4. To blaspheme the Vedic literature or literature in pursuance of the Vedic version.
5. To consider the glories of chanting Hare Krishna as imagination.
6. To give mundane interpretation of the holy name of the Lord.
7. To commit sinful activities on the strength of chanting the holy names of the Lord.
8. To consider the chanting of Hare Krishna as one of the auspicious, ritualistic activities which are offered in the *Vedas* as fruitive activities (*karma-kanda*).
9. To instruct a faithless person about the glories of the holy name.
10. To not have complete faith in the chanting of the holy names and to maintain material attachments even after understanding so many instructions on this matter. It is also offensive to be inattentive while chanting.

By learning to avoid these ten offenses anyone will quickly achieve the desired success, which is Krishna *prema*.

One of the hardest of these offenses to give up is holding onto material attachments. This does not merely mean holding on to objects of desire, but to the idea of "me" and "mine," especially in regard to bodily designations of who and what we think we are. The main word in that last statement is "think," because keeping materialistic attachments is mostly a mental activity, like habitual thought patterns. We may think we are male or female, black or white, old or young, Russian or American, wealthy or poor, a celebrity or not, etc., but such designations in our mentality will only distract us from the path of devotion. These are only materialistic designations and are symptoms of spiritual immaturity, and deterrents to proper cultivation of devotional service and higher spiritual realizations. It is a sign that you still have not understood your spiritual identity as a soul within the body, which is a part and parcel of the Supreme Being, Krishna, and that you actually belong to the spiritual realm, not this limited and temporary world of constant cycles of birth and death. However, by taking instruction from the spiritual master and the Vedic texts, and continuing to chant the holy names, one will eventually rise above such concepts and can gradually enter the stage of purely chanting the holy names.

The only way one can attain the stage of offenseless chanting is to mix with other devotees and avoid bad association. By chanting with concentration in the association of devotees, the heart becomes pure and ignorance is destroyed, one becomes more enlightened, and the taste for chanting increases. By Krishna's mercy, the bhakti-yogi may take shelter of a pure devotee who has fully experienced the potencies of the holy names, and who can guide you along the path more effectively. Otherwise, a person may remain misguided and not advance as quickly.

This is why it is explained, "One has to learn about the beauty and transcendental position of the holy name of the Lord by hearing the revealed scriptures from the mouths of devotees. Nowhere else can we hear of the sweetness of the Lord's holy names." (*Cc.*Antya. 1.101 & purport as follows:)

"Sanatana Gosvami has forbidden us from hearing the holy name of Krishna chanted by non-Vaishnavas, such as professional actors or singers, for it will have no effect. It is like milk touched by the lips of a serpent, as stated in the *Padma Purana*:

Chapter Eight

*avashnava-mukhodgirnam
putam hari-kathamrtam
shravanam naiva kartavyam
sarpocchishtam yatha payaha"*

It is in this way that when the name's nature becomes clear to the yogi, Krishna's spiritual form can also appear along with the name. We must understand, "Therefore, that material senses cannot appreciate Krishna's holy name, form, qualities and pastimes. But when a conditioned soul is awakened to Krishna consciousness and renders service by using his tongue to chant the Lord's holy names and taste the remnants of the Lord's food [*prasadam*], the tongue is purified [which also affects one's consciousness], and one gradually comes to understand who Krishna really is." (*Bhakti-rasamrita-sindhu*, 1.2.234 & *Cc.* Madhya, 17.136)

Thus, the perception of Krishna in the name drives away the modes of material nature, and pure goodness appears, which then bestows the realization of Krishna's spiritual qualities. According to the purity of the chanting, the Lord's pastimes can now also appear in the pure heart of the devotee who has awakened his natural spiritual vision. At that time, the material world takes on a whole different perspective, and one can see the spiritual energy that exists all around us. Thus, when the purified tongue glorifies the Lord with *japa* or simple recitation of the names, the mind can see Krishna's form, the heart perceives Krishna's qualities, and the soul in trance sees Krishna's pastimes. Such pastimes may be the activities in Vrindavana, as described in such texts as the *Bhagavatam*, or in the fact that the whole process of creation and annihilation of the material universes is itself a pastime of Krishna. (*Sri Caitanya-Siksamrita*, p. 232-4)

Srila Bhaktivinoda Thakur explains the way in which we can reach pure chanting: "If the holy name is seriously chanted just once, even though impurely, or if it is simply heard without distraction, the sound penetrating within to the soul, then the living entity can be immediately liberated, regardless of his high or low caste. And beyond this, when the holy name is chanted in the clearing stage (*namabhasa*--the second stage when impurities are swept from the heart of the chanter), then the highest goal is attained after some delay. All the other auspicious and pious results, including liberation can be quite easily achieved, but the attainment of love of Godhead is suspended for a while. In the clearing stage of chanting, the *jiva* is absolved of all sins, and by following this path, he gradually reaches the highest stage of chanting: *shuddhanama* or the pure name. One obtains love of Krishna only after reaching this stage of pure chanting. When *namabhasa* is complete, all sins and *anarthas* (unwanted desires in the heart) are dissipated, and the devotee chants purely. Then *shuddhanama* (the name in pure goodness) offers the devotee the highest spiritual success: love of Krishna." (*Sri Harinama Cintamani*, p. 16)

When we reach the stage of pure chanting, it becomes a whole new experience of happiness and bliss. This is when we have a strong taste for chanting. Pure chanting is described in the *Srimad-Bhagavatam* (3.15.25), "Persons whose bodily features change in ecstasy and who breathe heavily and perspire due to hearing the glories of the Lord [or His holy names] are promoted to the kingdom of God, even though they do not care for meditation and other austerities. The kingdom of God is above the material universes, and it is desired by Brahma and other demigods."

Furthermore, when we can purely chant the holy name, its power is fully revealed by our perception of its spiritual qualities. When a person takes complete shelter of the holy names, he or she becomes the recipient of the treasure of Krishna *prema*, or intense and ecstatic love for God. Therefore, when we reach this stage of offenseless chanting, the bhakti-yogi becomes eligible to receive Krishna's causeless mercy. What happens is that his chanting quickly awards him the divine fruit of *bhava*, the first stage of love of God. In this way, the bhakti-yogi is promoted from being a *sadhaka* or simple practitioner to *bhava*, one who can experience spontaneous pure devotional service. From *bhava* comes *prema*, which is the mature fruit of pure loving devotion, the likes of which can allow the devotee to taste the same emotions of love as the residents of Krishna's supreme abode of Goloka Vrindavana. This is the result of offenseless chanting. (*Sri Harinam Cintamani*, p. 90-1)

That love is especially exhibited through our desire to increasingly associate with the Lord through His divine names, such as the Hare Krishna mantra. As we chant more purely, meaning without the offenses to the holy name, the name, which is Krishna's own vibrational form, will further awaken one's love for Krishna, and continue to propel one into that spiritual dimension. As Srila Bhaktivinoda Thakur has written in his song *Sharanagati*, "When the name is even slightly revealed, it shows me my own spiritual form and characteristics. It steals my mind and takes it to Krishna's side. When the name is fully revealed, it takes me directly to Vraja, where it shows me my personal role in the eternal pastimes."

This is the power of Krishna's names when we can chant purely. It takes us, by revelation, to see and act in the spiritual dimension in our own capacity in the eternal pastimes of Lord Krishna. By becoming spiritually purified through the chanting of the holy names of Krishna, one's natural spiritual mood or *rasa* becomes revealed, which is the natural attraction for the soul to engage in loving exchanges with Krishna in a particular way. Thereafter, the devotee can meditate on doing service in that mood. If we have been cultivating a particular mood in our loving service to Krishna, the service and role we play in those pastimes of the spiritual world can also begin to be revealed by the power of the holy names.

This is greatly emphasized by Haridasa Thakur, the *acharya* of chanting the holy names. While discussing the glories of the holy name in an assembly of people in the village of Chandapura, Haridasa clearly explained that regardless of all the other benefits that can be attained by chanting the holy names of the Lord, by actually chanting the holy name without offenses, one awakens his ecstatic love for the lotus feet of Krishna. This is the ultimate purpose and goal. (*Cc*.Antya.3.178)

When the devotees become offenseless or qualified in the remembrance of Krishna's name, or concentration on His form, meditation on His qualities, absorption in His pastimes, they can ultimately enter into the pastimes with the taste of Krishna *rasa*, or a relationship with Krishna in a trance-like state. This is *apana-dasa*, remembering the various pastimes of Krishna in the eight different times of the day. When the devotees become deeply absorbed in this practice, they attain their *svarupa-siddhi*, which is the attainment of their eternal spiritual form and identity. These devotees can then be known as natural *paramahamsas*, swan-like devotees who have attained their natural spiritual identity. By the mercy of Krishna, when such devotees leave their material body at the time of death, they become associates of Krishna in the Vraja or Vrindavana pastimes in their own spiritual body. This is called *vastu-siddhi*. This is the ultimate result of purely chanting the holy names of Krishna, which is called *prapana-dasa*. (*Sri Caitanya-Siksamrita*, pp. 230-2)

This is how the process of chanting the holy names works, from the stage of merely trying it, then practicing it, and all the way up to the complete realization of one's spiritual identity.

PUTTING IT INTO PRACTICE

So how do we actually practice chanting the *maha-mantra*? First of all, there are no hard and fast rules for chanting the Hare Krishna *maha-mantra*. One can chant anywhere, anytime, in any situation. In fact, the *Caitanya-caritamrita* (Antya-lila, 20.18) describes that chanting the holy name at any time or place, even during sleep or while eating, brings one all perfection.

The proper way to chant is to give up all of our internal thoughts. As mentioned before, it is almost impossible to meditate on the void and empty our mind of all thinking. Our mind is always being pulled here and there by something. But the chanting process is easy because we simply concentrate on the mantra. However, our meditation on the mantra will be most effective if we can avoid the internal dialogue we always have within our mind. We should not be chanting while we make plans for the day, or while focusing our attention on other things. The *maha-mantra* is the Supreme in the incarnation of sound. Therefore, we must chant with complete respect and veneration. We must give the mantra our full attention, otherwise the chanting is considered offensive. The process is to simply chant and hear. That is all. If we can do that, then we will make rapid progress and quickly attain the second stage of chanting, which is the clearing stage.

As one progresses through the second stage, a person begins to get a taste for the chanting, and begins to feel the nectar of joy and bliss within the names. As a person enters the third or pure stage of chanting, the layers of ignorance that keeps one from realizing their spiritual identity are peeled away. At the fullest point, one gains direct perception of their spiritual identity and relationship with God, and is immediately liberated while still in the material body. The Lord reveals Himself to such a sincere devotee and the devotee relishes the taste of transcendental life. As Srila Rupa Gosvami states in his *Sri Upadesamrita* (text 7), everything about Krishna is spiritually sweet, such as His names, qualities and activities. But one who suffers from the disease of ignorance cannot taste this sweetness. Yet by chanting the names everyday, a person can destroy this disease and relish the natural sweetness of Krishna's names.

The Hare Krishna mantra is said to contain everything for both material and spiritual well-being. So if one chants Hare Krishna with material desires, he can attain these, as long as they are not too contrary to one's real well-being. And if one wants *mukti*, or liberation from the material world, he can also get that. Then again if one chants the Hare Krishna *maha-mantra* understanding that Radha and Krishna are personally present there, enjoying intimate pastimes in Vrindavana, then one can attain Their eternal loving service. Ultimately, the content of the mantra cannot be separated from the *sadhaka's* or practitioner's mentality. Both have a part to play at what will be attained through the use of it.

The essential state of mind that one should have while chanting the *maha-mantra* is described by Sri Chaitanya Mahaprabhu Himself in the third verse of His *Siksastaka* prayers:

> One should chant the holy name of the Lord in a humble state of mind, thinking oneself lower than the straw in the street; one should be more tolerant than a tree, devoid of all sense of false prestige and should be ready to offer all respect to others. In such a state of mind one can chant the holy name of the Lord constantly.

The names of God come directly from the spiritual world, Vaikuntha, which means the place of no anxiety. Therefore, the more we are absorbed in *kuntha*, or anxiety caused by material pursuits, the longer it will take for us to reach the Vaikuntha platform. But the more we associate with the Vaikuntha vibration of the *maha-mantra*, the sooner we will progress to the stage of experiencing the ecstasy that comes from awakening our transcendental love for the Supreme. The *Caitanya-caritamrita* (Adi-lila, 8.27) confirms that bodily transformations of spiritual ecstasy, such as trembling, perspiration, a faltering voice, and tears, may manifest when one's spiritual love for the Lord is actually awakened.

To begin progressing on the path of chanting the *maha-mantra*, it is prescribed that the practitioner chant on beads called *japa-mala*, similar to a rosary. This consists of 108 beads with one extra head bead, which is larger than the others. This represents the 108 *Upanishads*, or, as described elsewhere, Krishna in the form of the head bead surrounded by 108 of His most advanced devotees, the *gopis* of Vrindavana.

You may be able to purchase a set of *japa* beads at certain import shops or temples, or in India. If you cannot find them anywhere, you can also make them. Simply go to a crafts shop and purchase 108 beads of the same size and one larger bead of your choice for the Krishna bead. Also get a length of durable cotton or nylon cord. String all 108 beads with a knot in between each bead and bring the two ends of the cord through one hole of the Krishna bead and out the other side where you tie the two ends of the cord together in a firm knot. Then cut the remaining lengths of the cord so you have a small tassel. Now you have got your own set of beads for *japa* meditation.

A person chants the Hare Krishna mantra once on each bead from the head bead all the way around the 108 beads. This is one round, or one *mala*. Then without chanting on the Krishna bead, turn the beads around in your hand and go in the opposite direction and chant another round. One should set a certain amount of time each day, preferably in the morning, to peacefully sit down or walk and chant the particular number of rounds you have set for yourself. One may chant two rounds, four rounds, or whatever one can do.

For those who are serious, it is prescribed that they chant a total of at least sixteen rounds everyday. With a little practice, this normally takes about two hours. Two rounds will take about fifteen minutes. But one should set a fixed number of rounds to chant everyday. Then one can also spend some time reading spiritual texts, such as *Bhagavad-gita* or *Srimad-Bhagavatam* to enhance his or her spiritual development. A daily program of chanting and reading will produce definite results very quickly.

As with any form of meditation, it is best to do your chanting in the early morning when it is quiet and peaceful, and before your mind starts with the activities of the day. However, you can do it anytime or even at a few different times, such as in the morning and again in the evening to put things back into perspective, especially if you have had a busy or difficult day.

When you are ready to use the mantra, it does not hurt to calm the mind through the basic steps of preparation for meditation such as a few *pranayama* breathing techniques and so on. This is, after all, steps for preparing to attain deeper levels of awareness and consciousness, although this may not be necessary but can be helpful. Then take your *japa* beads and begin intently chanting the Hare Krishna mantra. When the mind is calm and focused, it especially will be able to concentrate on the vibrations of the mantra. As you chant it with your voice, it is received through the ear and considered by the intelligence. From there it goes deeper into the consciousness. Let no other thoughts enter the mind so that the mantra is all there is. Dive deep into the sound of your chanting and feel the vibration of the holy names and the divine energy they emit.

As you become regulated at this, doing it everyday, changes will begin to manifest in your consciousness that may be imperceptible at first, while other changes begin that will be noticeable from the start. You will often notice an internal energy within you that was not there before. Amongst other things, you may feel more sure of your own position and purpose in life, and a closer affinity with God and all beings. Of course, this is just the beginning, so if you do this regularly, deeper insights and realizations will occur as your consciousness acquires more clarity and purification.

CONCLUSION

This book contains descriptions of the glories and effectiveness of chanting the *maha-mantra*. Those who are intelligent will certainly add this spiritual practice to their lives. By taking it seriously, they will soon notice a change in their disposition. They may feel more peaceful, content, happy, etc. One trait that is always noticeable in a person who seriously takes to bhakti-yoga and the chanting of the *maha-mantra* is a decrease in such feelings as anxiety and distress, up to the point of complete fearlessness. Once someone is no longer afraid of death, then what is there to be afraid of in this material world? One loses such fear when he or she is spiritually Self-realized and knows he or she is not this body and, therefore, not actually subject to death, but merely undergoes a transformation of giving up the body. And by taking shelter of the protection of the holy names of Krishna, one will remain spiritually safe in any condition of life.

It is unfortunate that many people in the world are either not aware of this transcendental knowledge or have no taste for it. For such people, extensive material engagements and plan-making are their primary occupation. But this kind of activity is like working hard for nothing because in the end one is awarded only with death, in which all material assets are lost. As stated in *Srimad-Bhagavatam* (3.9.10), nondevotees engage in very troublesome work and cannot sleep well at night because they are absorbed in worldly plans. By providence their ambitions are frustrated and they continue in the cycle of repeated birth and death in material existence.

The only way, therefore, to get release from such material problems and be free from the contamination of the age of Kali-yuga is to take up the practice of bhakti-yoga and regularly chant the Hare Krishna *maha-mantra* while observing the regulations as best as one can. By chanting the *maha-mantra* with faith, a person will eventually purify his or her consciousness and reach success. As more people begin to chant the holy names, the troubles and upheavals found everywhere in the world will diminish, and this age of Kali-yuga can become like the peaceful and bountiful Satya-yuga-- the golden age. This is actually the prediction made by Lord Sri Chaitanya Mahaprabhu, who said that love of God will one day inundate the world and drown everyone, regardless of who or what they are. (*Caitanya-caritamrita*, Adi-lila, 7.26) Then many beneficial changes in this world will be seen. Therefore, the best thing any of us can do is to take it seriously.

> Let there be all victory for the chanting of the holy name of Lord Krishna, which can cleanse the mirror of the heart and stop the miseries of the blazing fire of material existence. That chanting is the waxing moon that spreads the white lotus of good fortune for all living entities. It is the life and soul of all education. The chanting of the holy name of Krishna expands the blissful ocean of transcendental life. It gives a cooling effect to everyone and enables one to taste full nectar at every step. (*Siksastaka* 1, written by Sri Chaitanya Mahaprabhu)

CHAPTER NINE

God Inaugurates the Maha-Mantra

The *Sri Caitanya Upanishad* (texts 5-11) of the *Atharva-veda* explains that one day when Pippalada asked his father, Lord Brahma, how the sinful living entities will be delivered in Kali-yuga and who should be the object of their worship and what mantra should they chant to be delivered, Brahma told him to listen carefully and he would describe what will take place in the age of Kali. Brahma said that the Supreme Lord Govinda, Krishna, will appear again in Kali-yuga as His own devotee in a two-armed form with a golden complexion in the area of Navadvipa along the Ganges. He will spread the system of devotional service and the chanting of the names of Krishna, especially in the form of the Hare Krishna *maha-mantra*; Hare Krishna, Hare Krishna, Krishna Krishna, Hare Hare / Hare Rama, Hare Rama, Rama Rama, Hare Hare.

Thus, it is further described that, "Accompanied by His personal devotees, Lord Krishna, assuming a golden color, introduces the *hari-nama-sankirtana*, the chanting of the Hare Krishna mantra, in the age of Kali. By this process, He delivers love for Krishna to the general populace.

"Lord Krishna, the son of Nanda Maharaja, personally introduces the occupational duty of the age of Kali. He personally chants and dances in ecstatic love, and thus the entire world chants congregationally." (*Cc.* Madhya. 20.341-2) This is the description of Sri Chaitanya Mahaprabhu who appeared in this world, in the area of Navadvipa, India, around 500 years ago.

So, we should not think that *sankirtana*, the group chanting of the Lord's holy names, is simply part of the system of mantra-yoga, or is merely a formula that has been passed down through the ages like other yoga systems. Nor is it a ritual, ceremony, or activity meant for producing good karma or positive fruitive results. Neither is it merely a way to focus the mind and achieve peace and tranquility. It is more than any of these.

As previously explained, there is a system of self-realization especially recommended for each age. In the age of Kali, people are not attracted to spiritual pursuits and are often rebellious against anything that seems to restrict or stifle their freedom to do anything they want. Since in this age we are so easily distracted by so many things and our mind is always in a whirl, we need an easy path. Therefore, the Vedic *shastra* explains that God has given us an easy way to return to Him in this age. It is almost as if He has said, "Since you are My worst son, I give you the easiest process." The *Caitanya-caritamrita* (Adi-lila, 3.40) confirms this and says that the Supreme Being descends as Sri Chaitanya, with a golden complexion, to simply spread the glories of chanting the holy names, which is the highest religious principle in this age of Kali. In this way, God Himself has given the method of chanting His holy names as the most effective means to reach His spiritual abode.

The Lord always descends to establish the codes of religion. This is confirmed in *Bhagavad-gita* (4.6-8) where Lord Krishna explains that although He is unborn and the Lord of all living beings, He still descends in His spiritual form to re-establish proper religious principles and annihilate the miscreants whenever there is a decline of religion and a rise in irreligious activity.

Though there are many incarnations or avatars of God, all avatars are known and predicted in the Vedic literature.

Each incarnation performs many wonderful pastimes. But in Kali-yuga the Lord descends as His own devotee in the form of Sri Chaitanya in order to show the perfect example of how devotional service should be performed, and to stress the chanting of the Hare Krishna mantra for this age by inaugurating the process of the *sankirtana* movement.

Therefore, Sri Chaitanya Mahaprabhu (February 27, 1486 to 1534 A.D.) was born in Navadvipa, Bengal, on a full moon night during a lunar eclipse. It is typical for people to bathe in the Ganges during an eclipse and chant the Lord's holy names for spiritual purification. So, everyone in the area was chanting the holy names when He was born. His parents, Jagannatha Misra and Sachidevi, gave Him the name of Vishvambhara, meaning the support of the universe, because astrologers had predicted His super human qualities and that He would deliver the people of the world. He was also nicknamed Nimai because He had been born under a nima tree.

During His childhood He exhibited extraordinary qualities, even having philosophical discussions with His mother. While growing, His brilliant intelligence began to become apparent. While still a child, He mastered Sanskrit and logic to the point of defeating local pundits, and established the truth of His spiritual and Vedic philosophy. He became so well known that many logicians of various religious and philosophical persuasions began to fear His presence and refused to debate with Him. Thus, Sri Chaitanya established the authority of the Vaishnava tradition through the process of debate and logic.

Then, when Sri Chaitanya went to Gaya on the pretext to perform ceremonies for the anniversary of His father's death, He received Vaishnava initiation from Ishvara Puri. Thereafter, He lost all interest in debate and simply absorbed Himself in chanting and singing the names of Lord Krishna in devotional ecstasy. Upon returning to Navadvipa, He gathered a following with whom He would engage in congregational singing of the Lord's holy names. Thus, He started the first *sankirtana* (congregational devotional singing) movement, and established the importance of chanting the names of God in this age as the most elevated of spiritual processes, and the prime means for liberation from material attachments.

At first, His chanting with people was for the few participants who were a part of His group, but then Sri Chaitanya ordered that the ecstasy of love of God be distributed to all people of the area. He gave no recognition for the privileges of caste, or for position, or type of philosophy a person had, or yogic asceticism. He only emphasized the devotional chanting of the Lord's holy names, using the Hare Krishna mantra (Hare Krishna, Hare Krishna, Krishna Krishna, Hare Hare / Hare Rama, Hare Rama, Rama Rama, Hare Hare) which can bring out the natural loving sentiments for God.

It was at the age of 24 when He shaved His head and took the order of sannyasa, the renounced stage of life, when He accepted the name of Krishna Chaitanya from Keshava Bharati during the initiation. He then spent four years traveling through South India, and also visited Vrindavana and Varanasi. During this time he also gave special instructions to Rupa and Sanatana Gosvamis, who then also spread the glories of the Divine Love for Radha and Krishna. They settled in Vrindavana where they spent their years in writing many books elaborating the instructions of Lord Chaitanya and the glories of bhakti for Radha and Krishna. They also revealed the places where Radha and Krishna performed many varied pastimes in that land of Vrindavana, which have remained special spots where devotees can become absorbed in the bliss of love of Radha and Krishna.

Lord Chaitanya spent His remaining years in Jagannatha Puri. During this time He was absorbed in ecstatic devotion to Krishna in the loving mood of Radharani, in which He would lose all external consciousness. He freely distributed the divine nectar of this love for Krishna to everyone and anyone, day and night. Even His presence or mere touch could transform everyone that came near Him into the same devotional mood. He remained like this until He finally left our vision at the age of 48.

Some of the predictions of the appearance of Lord Chaitanya can be found in many Vedic texts. One of them is from the *Svetasvatara Upanishad* (3.12): "The Supreme Personality of God [Purusha] is Mahaprabhu [great master], the propagator of transcendental enlightenment." Another is from the *Vayu Purana*: "In the age of Kali I shall descend as the son of Sacidevi to inaugurate the *sankirtana* movement." The *Bhagavatam* (11.5.32) also describes how intelligent men sing the holy names to worship the incarnation of God who is accompanied by His associates and always sings the names of Krishna. And in *Caitanya-caritamrita* (Adi-lila, 3.19-20) the Supreme Lord Himself describes how He will appear as His own devotee to perform and teach devotional service by inaugurating the *sankirtana* movement, which is the religion for this age.

The great classic *Mahabharata* (Vishnu-sahasra-nama-stotra, 127.92.75) confirms that Sri Chaitanya Mahaprabhu is not different from Lord Sri Krishna: "The Supreme Lord has a golden complexion [when He appears as Lord Chaitanya]. Indeed, His entire body, which is very nicely constituted, is like molten gold. Sandalwood pulp is smeared all over His body. He will take the fourth order of life [sannyasa] and will be very self-controlled. He will be distinguished from Mayavadi sannyasis in that He will be fixed in devotional service and will propagate the *sankirtana* movement."

These and other predictions confirm the fact that Sri Chaitanya Mahaprabhu would appear to specifically propagate the chanting of the holy names. Of course, now we have complete descriptions and elaborations on His life, activities, and philosophy, as had been written by His close associates. This verifies the fact that the chanting of the *maha-mantra* is the rare and special opportunity given by God for all to be relieved from the problems of the age of Kali and of material life in general. As confirmed in the *Caitanya-caritamrita* (Adi-lila, 3.77-78), it is Sri Krishna Chaitanya who inaugurates the congregational chanting of the holy names, which is the most sublime of all spiritual sacrifices. Intelligent people will worship Him through this means, while other foolish people will continue in the cycle of repeated birth and death in this material world.

As spoken to Sri Chaitanya by His spiritual master: "'My dear child, continue dancing, chanting and performing *sankirtana* in association with devotees. Furthermore, go out and preach the value of chanting Krishna-*nama*, for by this process You will be able to deliver all fallen souls.' (*Cc.* Adi. 7.91)

In this way, Sri Chaitanya Mahaprabhu contributed the greatest benefit to the people of East Bengal by initiating them into *hari-nama*, the chanting of the Hare Krishna *maha-mantra*, and making them learned scholars by educating them." (*Cc.* Adi.16.19)

It is the repetition of this process by the pure devotees and the followers of such pure devotees that this chanting will spread. It is only by the spiritual purity and not by force or sly conversion tactics that the process of chanting Hare Krishna is taken up by others around the world. As explained herein, "When someone heard the chanting of the holy name from the mouth of Sri Chaitanya Mahaprabhu, and someone else heard this chanting from the second person, and someone again heard this chanting from the third person, everyone in all countries became a Vaishnava through such disciplic succession. Thus everyone chanted the holy name of Krishna and Hari, and they danced, cried and smiled." (*Cc.*Madhya-lila, 17.48-49)

Therefore, "The religious practice for the age of Kali is to broadcast the glories of the holy name. Only for this purpose has the Lord, in a yellow color, descended as Lord Chaitanya." (*Cc.*Adi-lila, 3.40)

In another place in the *Caitanya-caritamrita* (Antya-lila, 20.8-9) Sri Chaitanya specifically tells Svarupa Damodara and Ramananda Raya that chanting the holy names is the most practical way to attain salvation from material existence in this age, and anyone who is intelligent and takes up this process of worshiping Krishna will attain the direct shelter of Krishna.

This is the power and special nature of the *mahamantra*, to not only bring a person to complete spiritual realization, but to also pave the way by which such a person can enter into the spiritual realm, into the eternal pastimes of the Supreme.

CHAPTER TEN

The Holy Name is the Incarnation of God for the Age of Kali-Yuga

In the *Bhagavad-gita* (4.7), Sri Krishna clearly explains, "Whenever and wherever there is a decline in religious practice, O descendant of Bharata, and a predominant rise of irreligion–at that time I descend Myself."

From all that we have learned in the previous chapters about the holy name of the Lord, we can understand that during this age of Kali-yuga it is the holy name, especially in the form of the Hare Krishna mantra, that is the present incarnation of the Lord and His energy for this present age. Between the time of Sri Caitanya 500 years ago, and the next avatara of the Supreme in His form as Lord Kalki, who appears at the end of the age of Kali-yuga, who or what is there for us to take shelter? It is this maha-mantra, the holy sound of Hare Krishna. As the *Caitanya-caritamrta* (Adi-lila, 17.22) and the Padma Purana says, the Hare Krishna maha-mantra is the sound incarnation of Krishna, and anyone who chants this mantra is in direct association with Krishna and can be delivered from the clutches of the material energy.

So the names of the Lord are also the same energy of the Lord. They are identical. By chanting Hare Krishna we are in immediate contact with God. This is further elaborated in the *Caitanya-caritamrta* (Madhya-lila, 17.131-133), which explains that there is no difference between the Lord's name, form, or personality, and they are all transcendentally sweet.

Chapter Ten

Krishna's name is the same as Krishna Himself, and is not material in any way. It gives spiritual benedictions and is full of pleasure.

In this way, the more we engage in chanting these names, the more purified we become, and the more we can chant these names purely, or more spiritually. This means that as we become more spiritualized, the more the names can exhibit their true potency. Then the more we can derive the ultimate benefits from this transcendental sound vibration.

The point is, just as we can take shelter of the Lord when He is appearing in one of His forms on earth, we can also take shelter of His holy names. The holy name is the incarnation of the Lord in this age.

This also means that the more we associate with these names through any number of ways, the more positive effect they will have on us, both individually and socially. We can chant these names in japa meditation, quietly chanting for our own benefit, or we can chant these names in the congregational singing of them. Or we can also merely think about them and chant them in our mind. In any way we do this, they will bring about a spiritual effect. Of course, the more spiritualized we become, the more dynamic that effect will be.

For example, as we associate or practice the chanting of this maha-mantra, it will purify us from our bad habits, addictions, and negative thought patterns, and help us rise above the more debased tendencies that we may have. It will help us reach our higher potential, think more clearly, give us peace of mind, realize who we are and how best to live our life, and so on. It can also protect us from dark forces that may be lurking nearby, and that may try to pull us down into unwanted thoughts and activities or experiences. Socially, it will also raise the consciousness of humanity, help reduce the tendency toward crime, assaults, robberies, rapes, corruption, greed, lying, and so on. It will help put humanity on the right track. It can clear our consciousness so that we can recognize the various levels of the illusion around us, the basis of wicked activities, and show us how to be free of such things. Therefore, the sound of the holy names needs to be broadcast or chanted through the streets of towns and cities. This is easy when people gather in groups to do this and practice chanting together. It will bring a subtle and spiritual relief to those who hear it, and also help pave the way for a more positive future for society, and provide spiritual development for those who join in the chanting.

People may not think of it very seriously at first. The more materialistic people are, the less attractive they may be to something that is genuinely spiritual. But that is the diseased condition of a materialistically motivated society. They may stoop to any level to get more money, power, position, influence, and sensual pleasure. But the more spiritual a person becomes, the more he or she will see the futility and superficiality of such desires, which only keep one chasing a temporary dream like needing another fix from a drug for another temporary high. In the end, when the high is gone, you are still left with nothing. But the spiritual joy is free and only increases with one's experience with the spiritual dimension. The maha-mantra is the channel through which the spiritual dimension descends into this material world. Therefore, we need to take advantage of it in any way we can. Otherwise, the darkness of materialism, and any philosophy that is based or promotes such darkness, will only increase and drag humanity farther and farther away from any real happiness and constructive and progressive way of living.

For this reason, the importance of associating with the holy names cannot be emphasized enough. It is our choice whether to do so or not. God does not force this on anyone, but the information has been supplied by His arrangement that we should see that it is to our benefit to utilize this methodology and experience the power of the holy names in this Hare Krishna maha-manta. It is indeed the incarnation of the Lord in the easiest way for any of us to approach Him.

Chapter Ten

Anyone can chant this mantra. No one is restricted. We only need to give it a chance, then become steady at it and take it seriously. Then the name can begin to act in all kinds of ways.

Quite honestly, when I was younger I used to smoke cigarettes. But when I started chanting the holy names on a regular basis, which at the time was only for about 15 minutes a day, or two rounds of 108 names each, I felt an inner strength I had not felt before. I wondered what I should first do with this inner power. I decided I would give up smoking once and for all. And that is what I did. I put more concentration on chanting, felt a higher taste and strength, and gave up smoking and never looked back, and never started smoking again. This is a very simple example, for the holy names of the maha-mantra have the power to do much more than that, which I have also experienced. But this simple example shows what can be done and how the maha-mantra can help anyone in any number of ways.

So, if we all took to this association with the spiritual realm, then we can see how so many dark tendencies of humanity can be overcome, and how our higher abilities can be awakened. Our love, compassion, morals, empathy, kindness, sympathy, forgiveness, cooperation, managerial abilities, insights, and so on, can all increase, not just individually but also socially on a mass scale. It can change the world. And these names can give more power in a healthier and more natural way than whatever power can be obtained by any dark practices that promise to assist us for temporary material awards or benefits, which always have unwanted side effects or consequences. This is the power of the Hare Krishna maha-mantra through which we can associate with the Supreme Lord and experience the spiritual realm, and surround ourselves with it, and raise ourselves to a higher level of awareness.

GLOSSARY

Acarya--the spiritual master who sets the proper standard by his own example.

Acintya-bhedabheda-tattva--simultaneously one and different. The doctrine Lord Sri Caitanya taught referring to the Absolute as being both personal and impersonal.

Advaita--nondual, meaning that the Absolute Truth is one, and that there is no individuality between the Supreme Being and the individual souls which merge into oneness, the Brahman, when released from material existence. The philosophy taught by Sankaracharya.

Agnihotra--the Vedic sacrifice in which offerings were made to the fire, such as ghee, milk, sesame seeds, grains, etc. The demigod Agni would deliver the offerings to the demigods that are referred to in the ritual.

Ahankara--false ego, identification with matter.

Ahimsa--nonviolence.

Akarma--actions which cause no *karmic* reactions.

Akasha--the ether, or etheric plane; a subtle material element in which sound travels.

Amrita--the nectar of immortality derived from churning the ocean of milk.

Ananda--spiritual bliss.

Ananta--unlimited.

Anuraga--That raga which makes the object of love experienced in ever-fresh ways and itself becomes ever-fresh; gives an experience of the hero with his form, qualities and sweetness, as if previously inexperienced; transforms by special thirst; experienced as if not experienced before. It is based on extreme strength of thirst and produces the perception of an object's absence when it is present.

Apana-dasa--The stage of accepting one's spiritual form (also called prapti)

Glossary

Apara-prakrti--the material energy of the Lord.

Aranyaka--sacred writings that are supposed to frame the essence of the *Upanishads*.

Arati--the ceremony of worship when incense and ghee lamps are offered to the Deities.

Arca-vigraha--the worshipable Deity form of the Lord made of stone, wood, etc.

Aryan--a noble person, one who is on the Vedic path of spiritual advancement.

Asana--postures for meditation, or exercises for developing the body into a fit instrument for spiritual advancement.

Asat--that which is temporary.

Ashrama--one of the four orders of spiritual life, such as *brahmacari* (celibate student), *grihastha* (married householder), *vanaprastha* (retired stage), and *sannyasa* (renunciate); or the abode of a spiritual teacher or *sadhu*.

Ashvamedha--a Vedic ritual involving offerings to God made by brahmana priests.

Astanga-yoga--the eightfold path of mystic yoga.

Asura--one who is ungodly or a demon.

Atma--the self or soul. Sometimes means the body, mind, and senses.

Atman--usually referred to as the Supreme Self.

Avatara--an incarnation of the Lord who descends from the spiritual world.

Avidya--ignorance or nescience.

Aum--*om* or *pranava*

Bhajan--song of worship.

Bhakta--a devotee of the Lord who is engaged in *bhakti-yoga*.

Bhakti--love and devotion for God.

Bhakti-yoga--the path of offering pure devotional service to the Supreme.

Bhava--Literally means that by which something is made known, or a transformation of the mind. A term generally used to convey specific moods, emotions, feelings and ecstatic experiences. A ray of *prema*, or preliminary *prema*. The first agitation of the heart in a developing sakhé as she matures.

Brahma--the demigod of creation who was born from Lord Vishnu, the first created living being and the engineer of the secondary stage of creation of the universe when all the living entities were manifested.

Brahmacari--a celibate student, usually five to twenty-five years of age, who is trained by the spiritual master. One of the four divisions or *ashramas* of spiritual life.

Brahmajyoti--the great white light or effulgence which emanates from the body of the Lord.

Brahmaloka--the highest planet or plane of existence in the universe; the planet where Lord Brahma lives.

Brahman--the spiritual energy; the all-pervading impersonal aspect of the Lord; or the Supreme Lord Himself.

Brahmana or brahmin--one of the four orders of society; the intellectual class of men who have been trained in the knowledge of the *Vedas* and initiated by a spiritual master.

Brahmana--the supplemental books of the four primary *Vedas*. They usually contained instructions for performing Vedic *agnihotras*, chanting the *mantras*, the purpose of the rituals, etc. The *Aitareya* and *Kaushitaki Brahmanas* belong to the *Rig-veda*, the *Satapatha Brahmana* belongs to the *White Yajur-veda*, and the *Taittiriya Brahmana* belongs to the *Black Yajur-veda*. The *Praudha* and *Shadvinsa Brahmanas* are two of the eight *Brahmanas* belonging to the *Atharva-veda*.

Caitanya-caritamrta--the scripture by Krishnadasa Kaviraja which explains the teachings and pastimes of Lord Chaitanya Mahaprabhu.

Candala--a person in the lowest class, or dog-eater.

Glossary

Chaitanya Mahaprabhu--the most recent incarnation of the Lord who appeared in the 15th century in Bengal and who originally started the *sankirtana* movement, based on congregational chanting of the holy names.

Chakra--a wheel, disk, or psychic energy center situated along the spinal column in the subtle body of the physical shell.

Chhandas--sacred hymns of the *Atharva-veda*.

Deity--the *arca-vigraha*, or worshipful form of the Divinity in the temple.

Deva--a demigod, or higher being.

Devas--demigods or heavenly beings from higher levels of material existence, or a godly person.

Dham--a holy place.

Dharma--the essential nature or duty of the living being.

Dualism--as related in this book, it refers to the Supreme as both an impersonal force (Brahman) as well as the Supreme Person.

Dwaita--dualism, the principle that the Absolute Truth consists of the infinite Supreme Being along with the infinitesimal, individual souls.

Gaudiya *sampradaya*--the school of Vaishnavism founded by Sri Caitanya.

Gayatri--the spiritual vibration or *mantra* from which the other *Vedas* were expanded and which is chanted by those who are initiated as *brahmanas* and given the spiritual understanding of Vedic philosophy.

Ghat--a bathing place along a river or lake with steps leading down to the water.

Goloka Vrindavana--the name of Lord Krishna's spiritual planet.

Gosvami--one who is master of the senses.

Govinda--a name of Krishna which means one who gives pleasure to the cows and senses.

Govindaraja--Krishna as Lord of the Cowherds.

Grihastha--the householder order of life. One of the four *ashramas* in spiritual life.

Hare--the Lord's pleasure potency, Radharani, who is approached for accessibility to the Lord.

Hari--a name of Krishna as the one who takes away one's obstacles on the spiritual path.

Haribol--a word that means to chant the name of the Lord, Hari.

Harinam--refers to the name of the Lord, Hari.

Impersonalism--the view that God has no personality or form, but is only an impersonal force (Brahman) which the individual souls merge back into when released from material existence.

Impersonalist--those who believe God has no personality or form.

Incarnation--the taking on of a body or form.

Japa--the chanting one performs, usually softly, for one's own meditation.

Japa-mala--the string of beads one uses for chanting.

Jiva--the individual soul or living being.

Jivanmukta--a liberated soul, though still in the material body and universe.

Jnana--knowledge which may be material or spiritual.

Jnana-kanda--the portion of the *Vedas* which stresses empirical speculation for understanding truth.

Jnana-yoga--the process of linking with the Supreme through empirical knowledge and mental speculation.

Jnani--one engaged in *jnana-yoga*, or the process of cultivating knowledge to understand the Absolute.

Kali-yuga--the fourth and present age, the age of quarrel and confusion, which lasts 432,000 years and began 5,000 years ago.

Kalki--future incarnation of Lord Vishnu who appears at the end of Kali-yuga.

Kalpa--a day in the life of Lord Brahma which lasts a thousand cycles of the four *yugas*.

Glossary

Kapila--an incarnation of Lord Krishna who propagated the Sankhya philosophy.

Karanodakasayi Vishnu (Maha-Vishnu)--the expansion of Lord Krishna who created all the material universes.

Karma--material actions performed in regard to developing one's position or for future results which produce *karmic* reactions. It is also the reactions one endures from such fruitive activities.

Karma-kanda--the portion of the *Vedas* which primarily deals with recommended fruitive activities for various results.

Karma-yoga--system of yoga for using one's activities for spiritual advancement.

Karmi--the fruitive worker, one who accumulates more *karma*.

Keshava--Krishna with long hair.

Kirtana--chanting or singing the glories of the Lord.

Krishna--the name of the original Supreme Personality of Godhead which means the most attractive and greatest pleasure. He is the source of all other incarnations, such as Vishnu, Rama, Narasimha, Narayana, Buddha.

Krishnaloka--the spiritual planet where Lord Krishna resides.

Kshatriya--the second class of *varna* of society, or occupation of administrative or protective service, such as warrior or military personnel.

Lakshmi--the goddess of fortune and wife of Lord Vishnu.

Lila--pastimes.

Lilavataras--the many incarnations of God who appear to display various spiritual pastimes to attract the conditioned souls in the material world.

Mahabharata--the great epic of the Pandavas, which includes the *Bhagavad-gita*, by Vyasadeva.

Maha-mantra--the best *mantra* for self-realization in this age, called the Hare Krishna *mantra*.

Mandir--a temple.

Mantra--a sound vibration which prepares the mind for spiritual realization and delivers the mind from material inclinations. In some cases a *mantra* is chanted for specific material benefits.

Maya--illusion, or anything that appears to not be connected with the eternal Absolute Truth.

Mayavadi--the impersonalist or voidist who believes that the Supreme has no form, or that any form of God is but a product of *maya*.

Mleccha--a derogatory name for an untouchable person, a meat-eater.

Moksha--liberation from material existence.

Om or *Omkara*--*pranava*, the transcendental *om mantra*, generally referring to the attributeless or impersonal aspects of the Absolute.

Paramahamsa--the highest level of self-realized devotees of the Lord.

Paramatma--the Supersoul, or localized expansion of the Lord.

Parampara--the system of disciplic succession through which transcendental knowledge descends.

Pranayama--control of the breathing process as in *astanga* or *raja-yoga*.

Pranava--same as *omkara*.

Prasada--food or other articles that have been offered to the Deity in the temple and then distributed amongst people as the blessings or mercy of the Deity.

Prema--Matured love for Krishna. Pure *rati* at the stage where only the Lord and nothing else is the subject, and is thus suitable for pastimes. When the relationship of love between the couple remains always without destruction even when there are causes for destroying it. When *bhava* become extremely condensed, it is called *prema*. It softens the heart completely and produces extreme possessiveness of the Lord in the experiencer. (BRS 1.4.1)

Glossary

Puja--the worship offered to the Deity.

Pujari--the priest who performs worship, *puja*, to the Deity.

Radha--Krishna's favorite devotee and the personification of His bliss potency.

Raga--Literally, attachment: an intense, irresistible, spontaneous absorption in, and attachment to, the object or person of one's attraction. A spontaneous deep thirst for the object of love. (BRS 1.2.272) The moods associated with this. More specifically, the stage of *prema* excelling *pranaya*, whereby suffering is removed by happiness in the heart on meeting Krishna. Or suffering becomes filled with happiness. The height of *raga* is when the height of suffering becomes filled with the height of enjoyment, meeting Krishna. When *anuraga* takes shelter of this "height of *raga*" it becomes *mahabhava*.

Raganuga-bhakti--That bhakti which follows after the *ragatmika bhakti* found distinctively in the residents of Vraja (BRS. 1.2.270) The person who is greedy for a *bhava* similar to that of the inhabitants of Vraja--who are fixed in *ragatmika bhakti*--is qualified for *raganuga* bhakti. (BRS 1.2.291)

Ragatmika-bhakti--Bhakti that is impelled exclusively by *raga* (deep spontaneous thirst for the object of love).

Rahu--deity representation of the planetary node that causes solar eclipses.

Sadhana--a specific practice or discipline for attaining God realization.

Sadhu--Indian holy man or devotee.

Samadhi--trance, the perfection of being absorbed in the Absolute.

Samsara--rounds of life; cycles of birth and death; reincarnation.

Sanatana-dharma--the eternal nature of the living being, to love and render service to the supreme lovable object, the Lord.

Sankirtana-yajna--the prescribed sacrifice for this age: congregational chanting of the holy names of God.

Sannyasa--the renounced order of life, the highest of the four *ashramas* on the spiritual path.

Satya-yuga--the first of the four ages which lasts 1,728,000 years.

Shabda-brahma--the original spiritual vibration or energy of which the *Vedas* are composed.

Shastra--the authentic revealed Vedic scripture.

Shiva--the benevolent one, the demigod who is in charge of the material mode of ignorance and the destruction of the universe. Part of the triad of Brahma, Vishnu, and Shiva who continually create, maintain, and destroy the universe. He is known as Rudra when displaying his destructive aspect.

Siddha-deha--The mentally conceived, perfect spiritual body, also known as *siddha-rupa* and *atma-svarupa*.

Smaranam--remembering the Lord.

Smriti--the traditional Vedic knowledge "that is remembered" from what was directly heard by or revealed to the *rishis*.

Sneha--Literally means "melting". *Prema* that ascends to its highest excellence, more fully illuminates the object of love, and liquefies the heart. When *sneha* arises, one can never be fully satisfied with seeing the Lord, nor can one tolerate even a moment's separation. (BRS 3.2.84).

Sravanam--hearing about the Lord.

Srimad-Bhagavatam--the most ripened fruit of the tree of Vedic knowledge compiled by Vyasadeva.

Sruti--scriptures that were received directly from God and transmitted orally by *brahmanas* or *rishis* down through succeeding generations. Traditionally, it is considered the four primary *Vedas*.

Sudra--the working class of society, the fourth of the *varnas*.

Svami--one who can control his mind and senses.

Glossary

Upanishads--the portions of the *Vedas* which primarily explain philosophically the Absolute Truth. It is knowledge of Brahman which releases one from the world and allows one to attain self-realization when received from a qualified teacher. Except for the *Isa Upanishad*, which is the 40th chapter of the *Vajasaneyi Samhita* of the *Sukla* (*White*) *Yajur-veda*, the *Upanishads* are connected to the four primary *Vedas*, generally found in the *Brahmanas*.

Vaikunthas--the planets located in the spiritual sky.

Vaishnava--a worshiper of the Supreme Lord Vishnu or Krishna and His expansions or incarnations.

Vaishnava-*aparadha*--an offense against a Vaisnava or devotee, which can negate all of one's spiritual progress.

Vastu-siddhi--The final spiritual body obtained by taking birth from a *nitya siddha gopi* an eternally perfect *gopi* in Krishna's earthly pastimes. The stage of identity transformation after *svarupa siddhi*, and before *sampatti siddhi*.

Vasudeva--Krishna.

Vayu--demigod of the air.

Vedanta-sutras--the philosophical conclusion of the four *Vedas*.

Vedas--generally means the four primary *samhitas; Rig, Yajur, Sama, Atharva*.

Vishnu--the expansion of Lord Krishna who enters into the material energy to create and maintain the cosmic world.

Vrindavana--the place where Lord Krishna displayed His village pastimes 5,000 years ago, and is considered to be part of the spiritual abode.

Vyasadeva--the incarnation of God who appeared as the greatest philosopher who compiled the main portions of the Vedic literature into written form.

REFERENCES

Agni Purana, translated by N. Gangadharan, Motilal Banarsidass, Delhi, 1984

Atharva-veda, translated by Devi Chand, Munshiram Manoharlal, Delhi, 1980

Bhagavad-gita As It Is, translated by A. C. Bhaktivedanta Swami, Bhaktivedanta Book Trust, New York/Los Angeles, 1972

Bhakti-rasamrita-sindhu, (Nectar of Devotion), translated by A. C. Bhaktivedanta Swami, Bhaktivedanta Book Trust, New York/Los Angeles, 1970

Bhakti Rasamarita Sindhu, by Srila Rupa Gosvami, trans. By Bhanu Swami, Sri Vaikuntha Enterprises, Chennai, 2003

Brahma Purana, edited by J.L.Shastri, Motilal Banarsidass, Delhi 1985

Brahmanda Purana, edited by J.L.Shastri, Motilal Banarsidass, 1983

Brahma-samhita, translated by Bhaktisiddhanta Sarasvati Gosvami Thakur, Bhaktivedanta Book Trust, New York/Los Angeles,

Brahma Sutras, Baladeva Vidyabhusana, translated by H. H. Bhanu Swami, 2013.

Brahma-Vaivarta Purana, translated by Shanti Lal Nagar, edited by Acharya Ramesh Chaturvedi, Parimal Publications, Delhi, 2005.

Brihad-vishnu Purana

Brihan-naradiya Purana

Brihadaranyaka Upanishad

Caitanya-caritamrta, translated by A. C. Bhaktivedanta Swami, Bhaktivedanta Book Trust, Los Angeles, 1974

Caitanya Upanisad, translated by Kusakratha dasa, Bala Books, New York, 1970

References

The Divine Name, Raghava Chaitanya das, Bombay, 1954

Garuda Purana, edited by J. L. Shastri, Motilal Barnasidass, Delhi, 1985

Gautamiya Tantra,

Gopal-tapani Upanishad, by Krsna Dvaipayana Vedavyasa, commentary by Visvanatha Cakravarti Thakura, translated by Bhumipati dasa, Ras Bihari Lal & Sons, Loi Bazaar, Vrindaban, UP, 281121, India, 2004

Hymns of the Rig-veda, tr. by Griffith, Motilal Banarsidass, Delhi, 1973

Kali-santarana Upanishad,

Krsna Sandarbha, Jiva Gosvamai, translated by H. H. Bhanu Swami, Sri Vaikuntha Enterprises, Chennai, India, 2014.

Mukunda-mala-stotra

Mundaka Upanishad,

Namamrta Samudra, Sri Narahari Cakravarti Thakur, translated by Bhumipati dasa, Rasbihari Lal & Sons, Vrindavan, India, 2004.

Narada-pancaratra,

Narada Pancharatram, Swami Vijnananand, Parimal Publications, Delhi, 1993

Narada Purana, tr. by Ganesh Vasudeo Tagare, Banarsidass, Delhi, 1980

Narada Sutras, translated by Hari Prasad Shastri, Shanti Sadan, London, 1963

Narada-Bhakti-Sutra, A. C. Bhaktivedanta Swami, Bhaktivedanta Book Trust, Los Angeles, 1991

Narasimha Purana,

The Nectar of Devotion, The Complete Science of Bhakti-yoga, A. C. Bhaktivedanta Swami Prabhupada, The Bhaktivedanta Book Trust, Los Angeles, 1970.

Padma Purana, tr. by S. Venkitasubramonia Iyer, Banarsidass, Delhi, 1988

Padyavali, Anthology of Devotional Poetry, Srila Rupa Gosvami, translated by Kusakratha dasa, Ras Bihari Lal & Sons, Loi Bazaar, Vrindaban, UP, 281121, India, 2007

Hymns of the Rig-veda, tr. by Griffith, Motilal Banarsidass, Delhi, 1973

Shri Chaitanya Mahaprabhu, His Life and Precepts, Thakur Bhakti Vinode, Sree Gaudiya Math, Madras, 1991

Siksastaka, of Sri Caitanya Mahaprabhu.

Skanda Purana, by Srila Vyasadeva, Purnaprajna Dasa, Rasbihari Lal & Sons, Vrindavana, India, 2005.

Sri Brihad-Bhagavatamrita, by Srila Sanatana Gosvami, trans. By Gopiparanadhana dasa, Bhaktivedanta Book Trust, Los Angeles, 2002.

Sri Brihat Bhagavatamritam, by Sri Srila Sanatana Gosvami, Sree Gaudiya Math, Madras, India, 1987

Sri Caitanya Bhagavat, by Sri Vrindavan dasa Thakura, 1538 AD.

Sri Caitanya-Bhagavat, by Sri Vrindavan dasa Thakura, trans. By Kusakratha dasa, Krsna Institute, Alachua, FL, 1994

Sri Caitanya Mangala, Locana Dasa Thakura, trans., by Subhag Swami, published by Mahanidhi Swami, Vrindavana, 1994

Sri Caitanya Shikshamritam, Thakura Bhakti Vinode, Sree Gaudiya Math, Madras, 1983

Sri Caitanya-siksamrta, The Nectarean Teachings of Sri Caitanya, Srila Bhaktivinoda Thakura, translated by H. H. Bhanu Swami, Brihat Mrdanga Press, Vrindavana, India, 2004

Sri Caitanya Upanishad, from the Atharva-veda

Sri Gopala-Tapani Upanishad, from the Atharva-Veda,

Sri Hari-bhakti-vilasa, Srila Sanatana Gosvami, translated by Bhumipati dasa, edited by Purnaprajna Dasa, Rasbihari Lal & Sons, Vrindavana, India, 2006.

References

Sri Harinam Cintamani, Srila Bhaktivinoda Thakura, trans. Sarvabhavana dasa, Bhaktivedanta Books, Mumbai, 1990

Srimad-Bhagavatam, translated by A. C. Bhaktivedanta Swami, Bhaktivedanta Book trust, New York/Los Angeles, 1972

Sri Narada Pancaratra, Vol. 1 & 2, Sri Krsna Dvaipayana Vyasa, translated by Bhumipati Dasa, Rasbihari Lal & Sons, Vrindavan, India, 2005.

Svetasvatara Upanishad, *Twelve Essential Upanishads*, Tridandi Sri Bhakti Prajnan Yati, Sree Gaudiya Math, Madras, 1982. Includes the *Isha, Kena, Katha, Prashna, Mundaka, Mandukya, Taittiriya, Aitareya, Chandogya, Brihadaranyaka, Svetasvatara,* and *Gopalatapani Upanishad* of the Pippalada section of the *Atharva-veda*.

Upadesamrta (Nectar of Instruction), translated by A. C. Bhaktivedanta Swami, Bhaktivedanta Book Trust, New York/Los Angeles, 1975

The Upanishads, translated by Swami Prabhavananda and Frederick Manchester, New American Library, New York, 1957; contains Katha, Isha, Kena, Prasna, Mundaka, Mandukya, Taittiriya, Aitareya, Chandogya, Brihadaranyaka, Kaivalya, and Svetasvatara Upanishads.

Vayu Purana, translated by G. V. Tagare, Banarsidass, Delhi, India, 1987

Vedanta-Sutras of Badarayana with Commentary of Baladeva Vidyabhusana, translated by Rai Bahadur Srisa Chandra Vasu, Munshiram Manoharlal, New Delhi, 1979.

Vishnu Purana, translated by H. H. Wilson, Nag Publishers, Delhi

INDEX

Ajamila
    the story of 24
Asanas
    promotes better health
    138
AUM
    meaning of 10
Being spiritual 138
Bija Mantras 5
Brahmastra 21
    a weapon formed by
    mantras 21
Chaitanya Mahaprabhu
    His appearance and
    purpose 105
    most recent avatar of
    God 105
Chanting
    most effective process
    102
Chanting Hare Krishna
    one can attain moksha
    77
Chanting the holy names
    God Himself has
    given this method
    102
    how to chant 94
    most practical and
    effective process 45
    uproots material
    desires in the
    heart. 28
Chanting Lord's names
    why it's so effective 43
Dhyana Mantras 5
Gayatri Mantras. 6
Hare Krishna
    how to chant 94
Hare Krishna maha-
    mantra 9, 36
    contains everything
    for well-being . 96
    frees one from
    material life. . . 77
    its meanings 33
    other processes are
    not necessary. . 44
    the process for
    chanting. 95
    vanquishes all sins. 76
Holy names
    most worshipable
    object. 76
    power of the Lords
    holy names . . . 64
    the most practical and
    effective process
    45
Incarnations of God. . 102
Japa 8
    meaning of the word 9
    quiet chanting
    meditation 4

Index

Japa-mala 97
Kali-yuga 46
  can become like
    Satya-yuga ... 100
  the process for this
    age 45
Krishna
  everything about Him
  is spiritually sweet
  95
Krishna's names
  their potency 43
Liberation
  through chanting .. 76
Maha-mantra
  how it works .. 19, 22
Mantra-yoga 3
  especially for this age
  3
Mantras
  different types 5
  means of doing
    different things . 3
  Sanskrit mantras ... 7
  used different ways . 8
Material existence
  to escape 76
Maya 14
Mula mantras 6
Nirguna mantras 8
Nirguna mantras 8
Om 10
  changeless supreme 10
  meditation technique
  16
Omkara 10

the om mantra 9
Pranama mantras 6
Pranava 10
Religion
  most important aspect
  78
Saguna mantras 8
Saguna mantras 8
Sankirtana 102
  congregational
    chanting 45
  most auspicious
    activity 27
Sanskrit mantras 7
Self-realization 22
Shabda-brahma
  Eternal spiritual
    vibration 5
Stutis and stotras 6
Vaikuntha 96
Vedas
  glorify Om 10
Vishnu
  potency of seeing
    Him 65
  the power of His
    name 48, 64
Vishnudutas 25
  soldiers of Lord
    Vishnu 25
Yamadutas 25
  soldiers of Yamaraja
  25
Yoga, benefits 138
  most important aspect
  78

ABOUT THE AUTHOR

Stephen Knapp grew up in a Christian family, during which time he seriously studied the Bible to understand its teachings. In his late teenage years, however, he sought answers to questions not easily explained in Christian theology. So he began to search through other religions and philosophies from around the world and started to find the answers for which he was looking. He also studied a variety of occult sciences, ancient mythology, mysticism, yoga, and the spiritual teachings of the East. After his first reading of the *Bhagavad-gita*, he felt he had found the last piece of the puzzle he had been putting together through all of his research. Therefore, he continued to study all of the major Vedic texts of India to gain a better understanding of the Vedic science.

It is known amongst all Eastern mystics that anyone, regardless of qualifications, academic or otherwise, who does not engage in the spiritual practices described in the Vedic texts cannot actually enter into understanding the depths of the Vedic spiritual science, nor acquire the realizations that should accompany it. So, rather than pursuing his research in an academic atmosphere at a university, Stephen directly engaged in the spiritual disciplines that have been recommended for hundreds of years. He continued his study of Vedic knowledge and spiritual practice under the guidance of a spiritual master. Through this process, and with the sanction of His Divine Grace A. C. Bhaktivedanta Swami Prabhupada, he became initiated into the genuine and authorized spiritual line of the Brahma-Madhava-Gaudiya *sampradaya*, which is a disciplic succession that descends back through Sri Caitanya Mahaprabhu and Sri Vyasadeva, the compiler of Vedic literature, and further back to Sri Krishna. At that time he was given the spiritual name of Sri

About the Author 129

Nandanandana dasa. In this way, he has been studying and practicing yoga since 1971, especially bhakti-yoga, and has attained many insights and realizations through this means. Besides being *brahminically* initiated, Stephen has also been to India more than 20 times and traveled extensively throughout the country, visiting most of the major holy places and gaining a wide variety of spiritual experiences that only such places can give. He has also spent nearly 40 years in the management of various Krishna temples.

Stephen has put the culmination of nearly 50 years of continuous research and travel experience into his books in an effort to share it with those who are also looking for spiritual understanding. More books are forthcoming, so stay in touch through his website to find out further developments.

More information about Stephen, his projects, books, free ebooks, and numerous articles and videos can be found on his website at: www.stephen-knapp.com or http://stephenknapp.info or his blog at http://stephenknapp.wordpress.com.

Stephen has continued to write books that include in *The Eastern Answers to the Mysteries of Life* series:
1. *The Secret Teachings of the Vedas: The Eastern Answers to the Mysteries of Life*
2. *The Universal Path to Enlightenment*
3. *The Vedic Prophecies: A New Look into the Future*
4. *How the Universe was Created and Our Purpose In It*
   He has also written:
5. *Toward World Peace: Seeing the Unity Between Us All*
6. *Facing Death: Welcoming the Afterlife*
7. *The Key to Real Happiness*
8. *Proof of Vedic Culture's Global Existence*
9. *The Heart of Hinduism: The Eastern Path to Freedom, Enlightenment and Illumination*
10. *The Power of the Dharma: An Introduction to Hinduism and Vedic Culture*
11. *Vedic Culture: The Difference it can Make in Your Life*

12. *Reincarnation & Karma: How They Really Affect Us*
13. *The Eleventh Commandment: The Next Step for Social Spiritual Development*
14. *Seeing Spiritual India: A Guide to Temples, Holy Sites, Festivals and Traditions*
15. *Crimes Against India: And the Need to Protect its Ancient Vedic Tradition*
16. *Yoga and Meditation: Their Real Purpose and How to Get Started*
17. *Avatars, Gods and Goddesses of Vedic Culture: Understanding the Characteristics, Powers and Positions of the Hindu Divinities*
18. *The Soul: Understanding Our Real Identity*
19. *Prayers, Mantras and Gayatris: A Collection for Insights, Protection, Spiritual Growth, and Many Other Blessings*
20. *Krishna Deities and Their Miracles: How the Images of Lord Krishna Interact with Their Devotees*
21. *Defending Vedic Dharma: Tackling the Issues to Make a Difference*
22. *Advancements of the Ancient Vedic Culture*
23. *Spreading Vedic Traditions Through Temples*
24. *The Bhakti-yoga Handbook*
25. *Lord Krishna and His Essential Teachings*
26. *Mysteries of the Ancient Vedic Empire*
27. *Casteism in India*
28. *Ancient History of Vedic Culture*
29. *A Complete Review of Vedic Literature*
30. *Destined for Infinity*, an exciting novel for those who prefer lighter reading, or learning spiritual knowledge in the context of an action oriented, spiritual adventure.
31. *Bhakti-Yoga: The Easy Path of Devotional Yoga.*

BOOKS BY STEPHEN KNAPP

If you have enjoyed this book, or if you are serious about finding higher levels of real spiritual Truth, and learning more about the mysteries of India's Vedic culture, then you will also want to get other books written by Stephen Knapp, a few of which include:

The Secret Teachings of the Vedas
The Eastern Answers to the Mysteries of Life

This book presents the essence of the ancient Eastern philosophy and summarizes some of the most elevated and important of all spiritual knowledge. This enlightening information is explained in a clear and concise way and is essential for all who want to increase their spiritual understanding, regardless of what their religious background may be. If you are looking for a book to give you an in-depth introduction to the Vedic spiritual knowledge, and to get you started in real spiritual understanding, this is the book!

The topics include: What is your real spiritual identity; the Vedic explanation of the soul; scientific evidence that consciousness is separate from but interacts with the body; the real unity between us all; how to attain the highest happiness and freedom from the cause of suffering; the law of karma and reincarnation; the karma of a nation; where you are really going in life; the real process of progressive evolution; life after death—heaven, hell, or beyond; a description of the spiritual realm; the nature of the Absolute Truth—personal God or impersonal force; recognizing the existence of the Supreme; the reason why we exist at all; and much more. This book provides the answers to questions not found in other religions or philosophies, and condenses information from a wide variety of sources that would take a person years to assemble. It also contains many quotations from the Vedic texts to let the texts speak for themselves, and to show the knowledge the Vedas have held for thousands of years. It also explains the history and origins of the Vedic literature. This book has been called one of the best reviews of Eastern philosophy available.

Trim size 6"x9", 320 pages, ISBN: 0-9617410-1-5, $14.95.

The Vedic Prophecies
A New Look into the Future

The Vedic prophecies take you to the end of time! This is the first book ever to present the unique predictions found in the ancient Vedic texts of India. These prophecies are like no others and will provide you with a very different view of the future and how things fit together in the plan for the universe.

Now you can discover the amazing secrets that are hidden in the oldest spiritual writings on the planet. Find out what they say about the distant future, and what the seers of long ago saw in their visions of the destiny of the world.

This book will reveal predictions of deteriorating social changes and how to avoid them; future droughts and famines; low-class rulers and evil governments; whether there will be another appearance (second coming) of God; and predictions of a new spiritual awareness and how it will spread around the world. You will also learn the answers to such questions as:

- Does the future get worse or better?
- Will there be future world wars or global disasters?
- What lies beyond the predictions of Nostradamus, the Mayan prophecies, or the Biblical apocalypse?
- Are we in the end times? How to recognize them if we are.
- Does the world come to an end? If so, when and how?

Now you can find out what the future holds. The Vedic Prophecies carry an important message and warning for all humanity, which needs to be understood now!

Trim size 6"x9", 325 pages, ISBN:0-9617410-4-X, $20.95.

Proof of Vedic Culture's Global Existence

This book provides evidence which makes it clear that the ancient Vedic culture was once a global society. Even today we can see its influence in any part of the world. No matter what we may consider our present religion, society or country, we are all descendants of this ancient global civilization. Thus, the Vedic culture is the parent of all humanity and the original ancestor of all religions. In this way, we all share a common heritage.

This book is an attempt to allow humanity to see more clearly its universal roots. This book provides a look into:

- How Vedic knowledge was given to humanity by the Supreme.
- The history and traditional source of the Vedas and Vedic Aryan society.
- Who were the original Vedic Aryans. How Vedic society was a global influence and what shattered this world-wide society. How Sanskrit faded from being a global language.
- Many scientific discoveries over the past several centuries are only rediscoveries of what the Vedic literature already knew.
- How the origins of world literature are found in India and Sanskrit.
- The links between the Vedic and other ancient cultures, such as the Sumerians, Persians, Egyptians, Romans, Greeks, and others.
- Links between the Vedic tradition and Judaism, Christianity, Islam, and Buddhism.
- How many of the western holy sites, churches, and mosques were once the sites of Vedic holy places and sacred shrines.
- The Vedic influence presently found in such countries as Britain, France, Russia, Greece, Israel, Arabia, China, Japan, and in areas of Scandinavia, the Middle East, Africa, the South Pacific, and the Americas.
- Uncovering the truth of India's history: Powerful evidence that shows how many mosques and Muslim buildings were once opulent Vedic temples, including the Taj Mahal, Delhi's Jama Masjid, Kutab Minar, as well as buildings in many other cities, such as Agra, Ahmedabad, Bijapur, etc.
- How there is presently a need to plan for the survival of Vedic culture.

This book is sure to provide some amazing facts and evidence about the truth of world history and the ancient, global Vedic Culture. This book has enough startling information and historical evidence to cause a major shift in the way we view religious history and the basis of world traditions.

This book is 6"x9" trim size, 431 pages, ISBN: 978-1-4392-4648-1, $20.99.

Destined for Infinity

Deep within the mystical and spiritual practices of India are doors that lead to various levels of both higher and lower planes of existence. Few people from the outside are ever able to enter into the depths of these practices to experience such levels of reality.

This is the story of the mystical adventure of a man, Roman West, who entered deep into the secrets of India where few other Westerners have been able to penetrate. While living with a master in the Himalayan foothills and traveling the mystical path that leads to the Infinite, he witnesses the amazing powers the mystics can achieve and undergoes some of the most unusual experiences of his life. Under the guidance of a master that he meets in the mountains, he gradually develops mystic abilities of his own and attains the sacred vision of the enlightened sages and enters the unfathomable realm of Infinity. However, his peaceful life in the hills comes to an abrupt end when he is unexpectedly forced to confront the powerful forces of darkness that have been unleashed by an evil Tantric priest to kill both Roman and his master. His only chance to defeat the intense forces of darkness depends on whatever spiritual strength he has been able to develop.

This story includes traditions and legends that have existed for hundreds and thousands of years. All of the philosophy, rituals, mystic powers, forms of meditation, and descriptions of the Absolute are authentic and taken from narrations found in many of the sacred books of the East, or gathered by the author from his own experiences in India and information from various sages themselves.

This book will prepare you to perceive the multi-dimensional realities that exist all around us, outside our sense perception. This is a book that will give you many insights into the broad possibilities of our life and purpose in this world.

Published by iUniverse.com, 255 pages, 6" x 9" trim size, $16.95, ISBN: 0-595-33959-X.

The Power of the Dharma
An Introduction to Hinduism and Vedic Culture

The Power of the Dharma offers you a concise and easy-to-understand overview of the essential principles and customs of Hinduism and the reasons for them. It provides many insights into the depth and value of the timeless wisdom of Vedic spirituality and why the Dharmic path has survived for so many hundreds of years. It reveals why the Dharma is presently enjoying a renaissance of an increasing number of interested people who are exploring its teachings and seeing what its many techniques of Self-discovery have to offer.

Herein you will find:
- Quotes by noteworthy people on the unique qualities of Hinduism
- Essential principles of the Vedic spiritual path
- Particular traits and customs of Hindu worship and explanations of them
- Descriptions of the main Yoga systems
- The significance and legends of the colorful Hindu festivals
- Benefits of Ayurveda, Vastu, Vedic astrology and gemology,
- Important insights of Dharmic life and how to begin.

The Dharmic path can provide you the means for attaining your own spiritual realizations and experiences. In this way it is as relevant today as it was thousands of years ago. This is the power of the Dharma since its universal teachings have something to offer anyone.

Published by iUniverse.com, 170 pages, 6" x 9" trim size, $16.95, ISBN: 0-595-39352-7.

Crimes Against India:
And the Need to Protect its Ancient Vedic Traditions

1000 Years of Attacks Against Hinduism and What to Do about It

India has one of the oldest and most dynamic cultures of the world. Yet, many people do not know of the many attacks, wars, atrocities and sacrifices that Indian people have had to undergo to protect and preserve their country and spiritual tradition over the centuries. Many people also do not know of the many ways in which this profound heritage is being attacked and threatened today, and what we can do about it. Therefore, some of the topics included are:

- How there is a war against Hinduism and its yoga culture.
- The weaknesses of India that allowed invaders to conquer her.
- Lessons from India's real history that should not be forgotten.
- The atrocities committed by the Muslim invaders, and how they tried to destroy Vedic culture and its many temples, and slaughtered thousands of Indian Hindus.
- How the British viciously exploited India and its people for its resources.
- How the cruelest of all Christian Inquisitions in Goa tortured and killed thousands of Hindus.
- Action plans for preserving and strengthening Vedic India.
- How all Hindus must stand up and be strong for Sanatana-dharma, and promote the cooperation and unity for a Global Vedic Community.

India is a most resilient country, and is presently becoming a great economic power in the world. It also has one of the oldest and dynamic cultures the world has ever known, but few people seem to understand the many trials and difficulties that the country has faced, or the present problems India is still forced to deal with in preserving the culture of the majority Hindus who live in the country. This is described in the real history of the country, which a decreasing number of people seem to recall.

Therefore, this book is to honor the efforts that have been shown by those in the past who fought and worked to protect India and its culture, and to help preserve India as the homeland of a living and dynamic Vedic tradition of Sanatana-dharma (the eternal path of duty and wisdom).

Available from iUniverse.com. 370 pages, $24.95, ISBN: 978-1-4401-1158-7.

Yoga and Meditation Their Real Purpose and How to Get Started

Yoga is a nonsectarian spiritual science that has been practiced and developed over thousands of years. The benefits of yoga are numerous. On the mental level it strengthens concentration, determination, and builds a stronger character that can more easily sustain various tensions in our lives for peace of mind. The assortment of *asanas* or postures also provide stronger health and keeps various diseases in check. They improve physical strength, endurance and flexibility. These are some of the goals of yoga.

Its ultimate purpose is to raise our consciousness to directly perceive the spiritual dimension. Then we can have our own spiritual experiences. The point is that the more spiritual we become, the more we can perceive that which is spiritual. As we develop and grow in this way through yoga, the questions about spiritual life are no longer a mystery to solve, but become a reality to experience. It becomes a practical part of our lives. This book will show you how to do that. Some of the topics include:

- Benefits of yoga
- The real purpose of yoga
- The types of yoga, such as Hatha yoga, Karma yoga, Raja and Astanga yogas, Kundalini yoga, Bhakti yoga, Mudra yoga, Mantra yoga, and others.
- The Chakras and Koshas
- Asanas and postures, and the Surya Namaskar
- Pranayama and breathing techniques for inner changes
- Deep meditation and how to proceed
- The methods for using mantras
- Attaining spiritual enlightenment, and much more

This book is 6"x9" trim size, $17.95, 240 pages, 32 illustration, ISBN: 1451553269.

Avatars, Gods and Goddesses of Vedic Culture

The Characteristics, Powers and Positions of the Hindu Divinities

Understanding the assorted Divinities or gods and goddesses of the Vedic or Hindu pantheon is not so difficult as some people may think when it is presented simply and effectively. And that is what you will find in this book. This will open you to many of the possibilities and potentials of the Vedic tradition, and show how it has been able to cater to and fulfill the spiritual needs and development of so many people since time immemorial. Here you will find there is something for everyone.

This takes you into the heart of the deep, Vedic spiritual knowledge of how to perceive the Absolute Truth, the Supreme and the various powers and agents of the universal creation. This explains the characteristics and nature of the Vedic Divinities and their purposes, powers, and the ways they influence and affect the natural energies of the universe. It also shows how they can assist us and that blessings from them can help our own spiritual and material development and potentialities, depending on what we need.

Some of the Vedic Divinities that will be explained include Lord Krishna, Vishnu, Their main avatars and expansions, along with Brahma, Shiva, Ganesh, Murugan, Surya, Hanuman, as well as the goddesses of Sri Radha, Durga, Sarasvati, Lakshmi, and others. This also presents explanations of their names, attributes, dress, weapons, instruments, the meaning of the Shiva lingam, and some of the legends and stories that are connected with them. This will certainly give you a new insight into the expansive nature of the Vedic tradition.

This book is: $17.95 retail, 230 pages, 11 black & white photos, ISBN: 1453613765, EAN: 9781453613764.

The Soul
Understanding Our Real Identity
The Key to Spiritual Awakening

This book provides a summarization of the most essential spiritual knowledge that will give you the key to spiritual awakening. The descriptions will give you greater insights and a new look at who and what you really are as a spiritual being.

The idea that we are more than merely these material bodies is pervasive. It is established in every religion and spiritual path in this world. However, many religions only hint at the details of this knowledge, but if we look around we will find that practically the deepest and clearest descriptions of the soul and its characteristics are found in the ancient Vedic texts of India.

Herein you will find some of the most insightful spiritual knowledge and wisdom known to mankind. Some of the topics include:

- How you are more than your body
- The purpose of life
- Spiritual ignorance of the soul is the basis of illusion and suffering
- The path of spiritual realization
- How the soul is eternal
- The unbounded nature of the soul
- What is the Supersoul
- Attaining direct spiritual perception and experience of our real identity

This book will give you a deeper look into the ancient wisdom of India's Vedic, spiritual culture, and the means to recognize your real identity.

This book is 5 1/2"x8 1/2" trim size, 130 pages, $7.95, ISBN: 1453733833.

Krishna Deities and Their Miracles
How the Images of Lord Krishna Interact with Their Devotees

This book helps reveal how the Deities of Krishna in the temple are but another channel through which the Divine can be better understood and perceived. In fact, the Deities Themselves can exhibit what some would call miracles in the way They reveal how the Divine accepts the Deity form. These miracles between the Deities of Krishna and His devotees happen in many different ways, and all the time. This is one process through which Krishna, or the Supreme Being, reveals Himself and the reality of His existence. Stories of such miracles or occurrences extend through the ages up to modern times, and all around the world. This book relates an assortment of these events to show how the images in the temples have manifested Their personality and character in various ways in Their pastimes with Their devotees, whether it be for developing their devotion, instructing them, or simply giving them His kindness, mercy or inspiration.

This book helps show that the Supreme Reality is a person who plays and exhibits His pastimes in any manner He likes. This is also why worship of the Deity in the temple has been and remains a primary means of increasing one's devotion and connection with the Supreme Being.

Besides presenting stories of the reciprocation that can exist between Krishna in His Deity form and the ordinary living beings, other topics include:
- The antiquity of devotion to the Deity in the Vedic tradition.
- Historical sites of ancient Deity worship.
- Scriptural instructions and references to Deity veneration.
- The difference between idols and Deities.
- What is darshan and the significance of Deities.
- Why God would even take the initiative to reveal Himself to His devotees and accept the position of being a Deity.

This book will give deeper insight into the unlimited personality and causeless benevolence of the Supreme, especially to those who become devoted to Him.

This book is 6"x9" trim size, 210 pages, $14.95, ISBN: 1463734298.

Advancements of Ancient India's Vedic Culture
The Planet's Earliest Civilization and How it Influenced the World

This book shows how the planet's earliest civilization lead the world in both material and spiritual progress. From the Vedic culture of ancient India thousands of years ago, we find for example the origins of mathematics, especially algebra and geometry, as well as early astronomy and planetary observations, many instances of which can be read in the historical Vedic texts. Medicine in Ayurveda was the first to prescribe herbs for the remedy of disease, surgical instruments for operations, and more.

Other developments that were far superior and ahead of the rest of the world included:
- Writing and language, especially the development of sophisticated Sanskrit;
- Metallurgy and making the best known steel at the time;
- Ship building and global maritime trade;
- Textiles and the dying of fabric for which India was known all over the world;
- Agricultural and botanical achievements;
- Precise Vedic arts in painting, dance and music;
- The educational systems and the most famous of the early universities, like Nalanda and Takshashila;
- The source of individual freedom and fair government, and the character and actions of rulers;
- Military and the earliest of martial arts;
- Along with some of the most intricate, deep and profound of all philosophies and spiritual paths, which became the basis of many religions that followed later around the world.

These and more are the developments that came from India, much of which has been forgotten, but should again be recognized as the heritage of the ancient Indian Vedic tradition that continues to inspire humanity.

This book is 6"x9" trim size, 350 pages, $20.95, ISBN: 1477607897.

The Bhakti-yoga Handbook
A Guide for Beginning the Essentials of Devotional Yoga

This book is a guide for anyone who wants to begin the practice of bhakti-yoga in a practical and effective way. This supplies the information, the principles, the regular activities or *sadhana*, and how to have the right attitude in applying ourselves to attain success on the path of bhakti-yoga, which is uniting with God through love and devotion.

This outlines a general schedule for our daily spiritual activities and a typical morning program as found in most Krishna temples that are centered around devotional yoga. In this way, you will find the explanations on how to begin our day and set our mind, what meditations to do, which spiritual texts are best to study, and how we can make most everything we do as part of bhakti-yoga. All of these can be adjusted in a way that can be practiced and applied by anyone by anyone regardless of whether you are in a temple ashrama or in your own home or apartment.

Such topics include:
- The secret of bhakti-yoga and its potency in this day and age,
- The essential morning practice, the best time for meditation,
- The standard songs and mantras that we can use, as applied in most Krishna temples,
- Understanding the basics of the Vedic spiritual philosophy, such as karma, reincarnation, the Vedic description of the soul, etc.,
- How Vedic culture is still as relevant today as ever,
- Who is Sri Krishna,
- How to chant the Hare Krishna mantra,
- Standards for temple etiquette,
- The nine processes of bhakti-yoga, a variety of activities from which anyone can utilize,
- How to make our career a part of the yoga process,
- How to turn our cooking into bhakti-yoga,
- How to set up a home altar or temple room, depending on what standard you wish to establish,
- How to take care of deities in our home, if we have Them,
- How to perform the basic ceremonies like arati,

All of the basics and effective applications to get started and continue with your practice of bhakti-yoga is supplied so you can progress in a steady way, from beginner to advanced.

This is 278 pages, $14.95, ISBN: 149030228X.

Lord Krishna and His Essential Teachings
If God Were to Tell You the Truth About Life, This Is It

If God were to tell you the truth about life, this is it, or as close to it as you are going to find. Often times we go through life and occasionally find ourselves confused about why are we here, or what we are supposed to do. That is normal when we do not have proper knowledge or guidance. But such insight is available if we know where to look for it.

Some of the most plentiful, prominent and clearly defined spiritual teachings of all are found in the Vedic tradition, especially those that have been given to us by Lord Sri Krishna Himself. He has provided some of the most elaborate, detailed and direct of all spiritual knowledge that can be acquired by anyone. Therefore, this book uses numerous verses of Lord Krishna's directions as found in the various Vedic texts, all divided according to topic. So here is the heart or essential spiritual message of what Lord Krishna has given for the benefit of all mankind so we can progress onward and upward from whatever position we may find ourselves in this material world.

Some of the topics include:
- Who is Krishna, evidence from the ancient texts
- The most secret of all knowledge about life
- The rarity of human birth
- The real purpose of this creation
- How to perceive our spiritual identity
- How to practice mystic yoga
- Description of the Supersoul
- The way to meditate
- How to be a spiritual person in this material world
- The highest levels of spiritual enlightenment
- How to follow the process of bhakti or devotional yoga
- How bhakti frees us from past karma
- The importance of *Bhagavad-gita* in this day and age, and much more.

The instructions of Lord Krishna are like the comforting nectar that can warm the heart and soothe the soul.

This is 290 pages, $18.95, ISBN: 1499655878

Mysteries of the Ancient Vedic Empire
Recognizing Vedic Contributions to Other Cultures Around the World

The Vedic culture is accepted by numerous scholars as one of the most sophisticated civilizations to appear after the last glacial period of 12,000 years ago. It developed in ancient India, and as the people populated the region, they also expanded and spread into other parts of the planet, taking much of their culture with them.

This book takes us on a journey through history and across many countries as we point out similarities and remnants of the Vedic tradition that remain there to this day. These include forms of art, philosophy, religion, architecture, temples, ways of living, and so on. Such countries include: Nepal, Burma, Cambodia, Thailand, Vietnam, Korea, Malaysia, Indonesia, Sri Lanka, Egypt, Africa, the Middle East, Iraq, Afghanistan, Syria, Central Asia, Greece, Italy, Germany, Russia, Ireland, Scandinavia, the Americas, and more.

This book also explains:

- How many religions in the world have features that clearly descended from the oldest form of spiritual knowledge and truth as found in Vedic Dharma.
- How Vedic Dharma is still relevant today and can help establish peace through its timeless spiritual wisdom.
- It also helps unravel and reveal the true nature of the Vedic civilization, and how and why it infiltrated and contributed to so many areas and cultures of the world.
- It also shows a mysterious side of history that few others have recognized.

This book will help anyone understand how the advanced nature of the Vedic civilization and its universal spiritual principles fit into the development of so many other cultures and still contributes to the upliftment of society today.

This book is the follow-up of a previous volume called Proof of Vedic Culture's Global Existence, but with completely different information and resources, as well as updates, written in a more academic style, using hundreds of references, quotes and notes to verify all the information that is used.

This book is 460 pages, 6" x 9" trim size, $22.95, ISBN - 10: 1514394855, ISBN - 13: 978-1514394854.

A Complete Review of Vedic Literature
India's Ancient Library of Spiritual Knowledge

The Vedic texts of India provide some of the highest levels of spiritual knowledge known to man. But it is not just one book, it is a complete library that offers explanations of many aspects of spiritual development, and of the Absolute Truth, or God. These also describe the processes by which a person can directly perceive and attain the Supreme and enter the spiritual realm.

This book shows how these many texts fit together, their divisions, the supplements, what information they contain, and their philosophical conclusions. The contents of this book include:
Understanding the Spiritual Truths in Vedic Literature;
If You are New to the Study of Vedic Culture;
The Four Primary Vedas;
The Brahmanas and Aranyakas;
The Upanishads;
The Upa-Vedas and Vedangas;
The Sutras and Supplements;
The Smritis;
The Vedanta and Vedanta-Sutras;
The Itihasas;
A Review of the Puranas;
The Srimad-Bhagavatam;
The Preeminent Nature of the Srimad-Bhagavatam;
Different Paths in the Vedic literature;
The Ultimate Path to the Absolute.

This book is 106 pages, 5 ½"x8 ½", Paperback $5.99, and Kindle Ebook $1.99. ISBN-10: 1547278862.

www.Stephen-Knapp.com
http://stephenknapp.info
http://stephenknapp.wordpress.com

Be sure to visit Stephen's web site. It provides lots of information on many spiritual aspects of Vedic and spiritual philosophy, and Indian culture for both beginners and the scholarly. You will find:

- All the descriptions and contents of Stephen's books, how to order them, and keep up with any new books or articles that he has written.
- Reviews and unsolicited letters from readers who have expressed their appreciation for his books, as well as his website.
- Free online booklets are also available for your use or distribution on meditation, why be a Hindu, how to start yoga, meditation, etc.
- Helpful prayers, mantras, gayatris, and devotional songs.
- Over two hundred enlightening articles that can help answer many questions about life, the process of spiritual development, the basics of the Vedic path, or how to broaden our spiritual awareness.
- Over 150 color photos taken by Stephen during his travels through India. There are also descriptions and 40 photos of the huge and amazing Kumbha Mela festival.
- Directories of many Krishna and Hindu temples around the world to help you locate one near you, where you can continue your experience along the Eastern path.
- Photographic exhibit of the Vedic influence in the Taj Mahal, questioning whether it was built by Shah Jahan or a pre-existing Vedic building.
- A large list of links to additional websites to help you continue your exploration of Eastern philosophy, or provide more information and news about India, Hinduism, ancient Vedic culture, Vaishnavism, Hare Krishna sites, travel, visas, catalogs for books and paraphernalia, holy places, etc.
- A large resource for vegetarian recipes, information on its benefits, how to get started, ethnic stores, or non-meat ingredients and supplies.
- A large "Krishna Darshan Art Gallery" of photos and prints of Krishna and Vedic divinities. You can also find a large collection of previously unpublished photos of His Divine Grace A. C. Bhaktivedanta Swami.

This site is made as a practical resource for your use and is continually being updated and expanded with more articles, resources, and information. Be sure to check it out.

Made in the USA
Las Vegas, NV
19 October 2023